Meet Me in the Middle

Charlotte Holt Clinebell

MEET ME IN / On Becoming
THE MIDDLE / Human Together

1817

HARPER & ROW, PUBLISHERS

New York, Evanston, San Francisco, London

For Howard
who is willing, most of the time,
to meet me in the middle

MEET ME IN THE MIDDLE. Copyright © 1973 by Charlotte Holt Clinebell. All rights reserved. Printed in the United States of America. No part of this book may be used or reproduced in any manner whatsoever without written permission except in the case of brief quotations embodied in critical articles and reviews. For information address Harper & Row, Publishers, Inc., 10 East 53rd Street, New York, N.Y. 10022. Published simultaneously in Canada by Fitzhenry & Whiteside Limited, Toronto.

FIRST EDITION

Library of Congress Cataloging in Publication Data

Clinebell, Charlotte H
  Meet me in the middle.
  Includes bibliographical references.
  1. Woman—Psychology. 2. Marriage. 3. Interpersonal relations. I. Title.
HQ1206. C55   301.41'76'33   72–11353
ISBN 0–06–061501–X

Acknowledgments

I want to express my thanks to many friends, students, and clients who have shared with me their lives as women and are part of this book.

Barbara Henckel has been long-suffering in her bouts with typing an often illegible manuscript and helpful in her criticism of the ideas.

My particular thanks go to Rachel Roy for her time-consuming, patient, and sensitive criticism of the manuscript, and to Nancy Goldsmith, whose understanding and experience with the issues has helped me to clarify my own struggle at many points.

I am grateful to my parents, Helen Clary Holt and Harvey J. Holt, for encouraging in me a lively curiosity and an independent spirit.

Most of all I am indebted to my husband for his constant moral support and painstaking commentary on the manuscript, and to my children, especially my daughter Susan, who have been willing to tolerate a "liberated" mother and have insisted that I keep the problem in perspective.

Contents

Prologue / Before I Begin . . .   ix

One / What Is a Woman?   1

Two / What Is a Man?   16

Three / Equal though Different   31

Four / Liberated Marriage   44

Five / Liberated Sex   62

Six / Liberated Childhood   77

Seven / Liberated Work   95

Eight / Sexism and Survival   108

Nine / Living with a "Liberated" Woman:
        A Response by Howard J. Clinebell, Jr.   120

Epilogue / What's a Woman to Do?   125

Prologue / Before I Begin

I thought it would be easy to write this book. There's so much I want to say. So I've everything laid out around me in perfect order. The typewriter is plugged in and the pencils are sharpened, my notes are arranged by chapters on one side of me and a few books for reference on the other. A hot cup of coffee is on a tray next to my typewriter; a few flames from last night's fire flutter encouragingly among the coals in the fireplace. I've had my breakfast and done my exercises and listened to the news. All is ready. Now I can begin. My fingers are poised over the typewriter keys . . .

But there goes the phone. I must answer it: it might be one of the children, an emergency! The doorbell rings: maybe it's special delivery! The dishwasher needs emptying! I really ought to put a load of towels into the machine! Is there enough bread for lunch? There are so many excuses to avoid writing. Partly, it's just hard work and I *want* to be distracted. Partly I'm uneasy about putting myself on paper for all to read. But mostly it is that in this house where I've been wife and mother for so many years, all the things that "need to be done" cry out to me, "Don't you feel *guilty* sitting at that typewriter when there's so much around here that ought to be done?" Yes, I do! That's what I'm trying to change! The change has already begun and is making a major difference in my life.

For it's true that after forty-five years of life, twenty-three of them married, twenty of them as the mother of three children, now grown, and then as a "career woman," I began to wonder who I was. "What will I be when I grow up?" Actually, without realizing it, I'd been asking those questions for a number of years. Before that, I *knew* who I was and what I would be: somebody's daughter, somebody's

wife, somebody's mother. There was a period of uncertainty between the daughter and the wife stages, when I knew I couldn't be
a taken-care-of little girl any more and wasn't sure I'd catch a man
who would take care of me! I remember the moments of panic—
suppose I didn't get married! Suppose no one asked me! What would
I do then? Become a missionary?

But I was lucky, or canny, or both. The right man did come along
and I did the right "feminine" things to catch him. And just in time!
I didn't even have to go to work between school and marriage,
though I was trained to teach so I'd have something to fall back on
if I didn't marry; and so that I'd be educated enough to be a good
wife and mother. I quickly and happily became somebody's wife,
and before long, somebody's mother. I loved all the somebodies. On
the whole, I was content. Underneath there were some other feelings, but it never occurred to me to wonder who I would be without
the somebodies to define my identity and give me my importance.

The years accumulated. What a wonderful husband I had. He
earned degrees, he wrote books, he got good jobs. Were not his
successes mine too? What if it sometimes seemed to me as though
he had all the fun. I had the children. Just see what a good mother
I could be! The years kept on accumulating. Suddenly I had a son
in high school. In *high school?* And beginning to talk about college
and going away from home. *Away from home?* But what about me?
I could see the handwriting on the wall. Soon they would all be gone,
and my career as a mother, for better and worse, would be obsolete.

Never mind. I had a good marriage. I'd never be obsolete as a wife.
But I had a busy, successful husband. He loved me but he loved his
work too. I couldn't expect him to fill the void of time and emotion
that the empty nest would bring.

So I went back to school, to prepare myself for that all-too-immi-
nent day when I wouldn't be needed as a mother any more. Surprisingly, I liked it. It was exciting and challenging and it opened many
new doors for me. Where had I been all my life? Was I enjoying it
too much? Some of my children were still at home and needed a
mother. And my husband, urging me to "fulfill myself," did like his

meals served to him and his shirts washed. I felt guilty when I got behind in my "rightful duties." Going to school is okay if you can keep the household running smoothly too, and keep everybody happy.

Well, I did finish school, and I did get a job, doing work that I love and am good at. The family survived, and so did the marriage, though there were times when we all wondered. All in all, I like my new career role and my continuing wife and, for a while yet, mother roles. But most of all I like my growing identity, uneasy though it is at times. That's the excitement I feel—not just what I'm doing with my life, but how I feel about myself. I feel good about being me. What woke me up? Lots of things I guess: my children growing up and starting to leave home; going back to school and rediscovering the outside world; hearing and reading about women's liberation; talking to women who were having some of the same feelings I was. All these things helped to raise my consciousness of my need for a new me. All my life I had defined myself around other people's expectations of me. Now I'm discovering my own expectations of myself. What *can* I do, what do I *want* to do, what is it to be *me?* For me, these are new and exciting questions, questions that make me wish I were twenty again. There is also some uncertainty. How do I know where these discoveries will take me?

Wherever I go these days, I seem to hear the same questions from other women—from my middle-aged friends who are returning to school or to work, or to volunteer or creative activities, from clients who come for help because of a vague or a violent discontent with their marriages or their lives in general, from women in groups to whom I speak and listen, from women students of all ages. "Isn't there more to life than this?" "What am I missing?" "Why isn't my marriage more satisfying?" And from younger women, "Can I have marriage and still be me?" "Can I have a career too?" "Is there something wrong with me if I don't want children? "Or marriage?" What if I want children and a life of my own besides?" "What if I *want* to be a housewife?" Other women I meet haven't started asking those questions yet, but many of them feel the undefined emptiness or longing or frustration in themselves that has led many of us to these questions.

Surprisingly, many men are asking questions too. Our lives as women and men are so closely interwoven that when one sex changes, the other must also change. So men are discovering along with women that they are not as content with the old ways as they thought they were. This book is an attempt to deal with some of those questions. It is written for those of you, women and men, who are looking for more satisfying, more growth-stimulating, more open ways of living and relating as women and men.

To be human is to be lonely. Much of our frantic activity is a way of trying to avoid that loneliness. But in the deepest sense we can never avoid it or overcome it. Sometimes, though, we can "bridge the unbridgeable gap between two separate human beings"* in a genuine meeting between woman and man, woman and woman, man and man, parent and child. There have always been people of both sexes who are able to touch minds and hearts and souls. With this book I mean to affirm whatever is important and meaningful in past and present ways of being human together. There are many kinds of successful relationships. But I also mean to suggest that with the potential revolution in changing roles there are unlimited opportunities for us to relate to each other in new and deeper ways as men and women.

The message of this book is that the traditional way of meeting between women and men is neither the most satisfying nor the most human way of meeting for either sex. The dominance-submission pattern, the one up–one down relationship, cannot provide the conditions for the most open, growing, sexually satisfying relationship a couple can develop. The view that women are weak and dependent by nature has meant that men must always be the strong, supportive, independent ones. It has meant that women are not free to be strong as men are not free to be weak. At its worst it means that women

*Abraham Maslow, *Motivation and Personality* (New York: Harper & Row, 1954), p. 250.

must be weak so that men can be strong. And that denies the strength and the full humanness of both sexes.

There is another way, a better one, and that is what the title of this book means. The "middle" is the place where both men and women can get their needs met, individually and together, without one sex always on the top and the other on the bottom. In the middle we can love and work together. I am saying to men, "Meet me in the middle! I am no longer willing to meet you anywhere else. I want to share the excitement and joy of life with you, but I'm no longer willing to be 'one down.' I need to meet you in the middle in order to be fully human—in order to be and do whatever is possible for me. You need to meet me in the middle for the same reasons."

And to women I am saying, "Hey, it's a whole new world. Don't be content any longer with the short end of the stick. Don't be content to use only a part of your personality and your capability. As women we are becoming increasingly free to choose our destiny. We can choose to stay at home or to go to work or both. We can be homemakers or policewomen or both. We can enter politics or raise flowers or work for peace. We are even beginning to awaken our long-sleeping sexuality as women. Now, if we're going to ask men to meet us in the middle, we've got to get to the middle ourselves.

It's not going to be easy. Old ways die hard. Our society does not support the new ways. It's difficult for women to give up the comfortable dependencies and take on new responsibilities. It's hard for men to give up the advantages and security of dominance in spite of its burdens. But it's only by meeting in the middle, by joining our free spirits in the struggle to become human together, that mutual fulfillment—sexual, emotional, intellectual, spiritual—can occur. Only in such mutually affirming relationships can we raise fully human children. Only in such relationships can we gain the inner resources to solve the massive problems that face humanity. For it's pretty obvious that men can't run the world alone. Neither can women! But we haven't tried doing it together. It's time we let each other out of the boxes marked MALE and FEMALE. That's what *Meet Me in the Middle* is all about. Not just for me and my identity, but for women and for men and for humankind.

How little we know yet what humans can become. We know even less about what becoming human together can mean. But we've come to a time when we have the opportunity and the challenge and the *necessity* to develop, self-consciously new ways of relating as women and men. What will the revolution in changing roles bring? Nobody knows. But I for one can't wait to find out.

One / What Is a Woman?

A long time ago, on my sixteenth or seventeenth birthday, someone sent me a poem called "What Is a Woman?" Though it is long since lost, I can still remember the message. It described in glowing detail the attributes of the "ideal woman." She is kind and gentle and quiet. Her voice is soft and soothing and well modulated. She never argues or raises her voice. She is never angry. She is always willing to listen. She is compliant and submissive. She makes others feel both comfortable and important. She never makes demands or pushes herself on others, but is always alert for the opportunity to serve someone else. She may be intelligent, but she knows she fulfills her womanhood best when she uses her mind in the service of others rather than for her own achievement. The ideal woman's chief calling is her home. Her chief joy is in making it a warm nest for her children and a refuge from worldly battles for her husband. They can always find tenderness and sympathy at home.

My poem said, too, that the ideal woman is lighthearted and gay. If she is ever troubled she keeps it to herself. She doesn't burden her husband and children, who've had a hard day in the world, with her cares. She is devout though, and when she's feeling blue or unhappy she can take her troubles to God who will give her the strength she needs to be what others expect her to be. The ideal woman is hard-working. "She rises while it is yet night," like that marvelous woman in Proverbs, to cook and sew and clean. Above all, according to my poem, she never complains. She is able to turn her chores into domestic graces. She thinks first of her family; if she thinks of herself at all it is to wonder how she can be a better wife and mother!

Is it possible that I took that poem seriously? I remember feeling inspired. It seemed such a marvelous goal. And it did remind me of the "good wife" in Proverbs whom I kept hearing about in Mother's Day sermons and was already hoping to emulate. I felt uneasy though. Could I ever aspire to such heights? Could I ever reach the pedestal around which my husband and children would "rise up and call me blessed"? I doubted it. But I could try.

The poem was exaggerated, of course. Nobody really expected a woman to be so perfect. I must have known that and I forgot about the poem. But I happened to think of it the other day while I was musing about my identity questions. Way down underneath I felt that my success as a woman and therefore as a human being depended on my being able to give to others rather than to take for myself. The assumption of the poem that a woman is successful only if she becomes wife and mother, no matter what else she does, also was and is an accurate reflection of society's predominant expectations.

So I became wife and mother, and then I struggled to meet my own desire for success as a woman by trying to meet everyone else's needs. I rarely "rose while it was yet night" unless the baby cried. But often I felt guilty when I did let some task go that might have been done in the middle of the night. Sometimes I read a book or magazine, but when I heard my husband arriving, I quickly whisked it under a cushion or back on the shelf so that he would not find me "idle" but "busy" with the ironing or cooking. And I felt *guilty* that I had been wasting time reading. I devised some ways of "wasting time" without feeling guilty! It seemed okay to read while nursing the baby, for example, a good way to make an extremely pleasurable experience even more pleasurable and even to prolong it. And of course, the radio and subsequently television offered some opportunities for recreation and enlightenment, such as it was, which could be indulged in while ironing, cooking, or cleaning.

But fundamentally my sense of well-being was derived from trying to keep everyone else happy. Then, if there was time, I could practice the piano or read a book or go to a meeting.

My husband says he never experienced me as submissive and cowed. Apparently I didn't behave that way outwardly. But I certainly felt that way underneath. He also says now that he probably took much of my "servant" behavior for granted and as "natural" for a woman. Some of those old feelings are still with me at times. Even this moment, as I write, I'm aware of a vague discomfort. If I let myself stay with the feeling, the sound of my husband banging away in the kitchen (it's his week for the shopping and cleaning up) comes to my ears. The "vague discomfort" is that old guilt still spooking around inside of me. Can it really be right for him to be tending the home fires while I use my typewriter and my brain?

In those early years of my wifing and mothering I was doing what I wanted to do. Much of the time I *was* happy and fulfilled, and I wouldn't give up those experiences as wife and mother for anything. But I also remember some vague feelings of jealousy toward my husband because of his freedom and the stimulating life he seemed to lead away from home. And I remember resenting that I had to feel guilty when I did something *I* wanted to do. But in those moments I thought something was wrong with me, that I wasn't quite measuring up as a wife and mother or I wouldn't feel jealousy and resentment. So then I felt guilty about my negative feelings!

Lately I've come to understand one reason that Mother's Day has always bothered me either vaguely or violently: I never felt I measured up to the "Holy, Holy, Holy" image it demands. Although I never let myself think such a thought then, I believe I had a sneaking suspicion that I didn't really want to be so selfless and perfect. Although I strove to be devout and sweet and lighthearted, and loyal and compliant and sensitive, and though I succeeded at some of those things some of the time, mostly I did not. I was often angry, often raised my voice at my husband or children, often was sulky or martyred or blue. I never learned to wax eloquent over waxed floors —at least unless someone else waxed them! Of course I felt guilty over my failures, but that didn't seem to make me do any better.

Furthermore, my family was not always happy. Whether or not I *was* responsible for their unhappiness, I *felt* responsible. The ideal woman keeps her family happy and successful. What an impossible burden to bear! It was impossible for the children too. They had to be happy in order for me to be a success! Of course, it didn't work.

What I realize now as I look back is that I wasn't such a bad wife or such a bad mother—though I made a lot of mistakes—or even such an inadequate woman. What I didn't do such a good job of was being *me*. And that was destructive not only for me, but for my children and husband, too. Now I know it was a mistake to try, however unconsciously, to fit into some long-standing definition of a woman—a definition reinforced by the current culture, by all our institutions, by our child-rearing practices, and by the behavior of both women and men. It's a mistake to try to fit *any* external pattern or definition, ancient or modern, of what is a woman.

It's true that there is a part of me that is tender and sweet (maybe even delicate!) and spiritual and sympathetic and compliant and dependent and unselfish and compassionate and nurturing and serving and anxious to please and be liked. But now I know that there's a very real part of me that is assertive and aggressive and self-seeking and strong and competent and intelligent and achieving. If only I had been able to use *that* side of me more fully instead of feeling guilty about it, I would have been a happier human being and a more honest one. Now I'm discovering it's not too late.

Another thing I've had to start overcoming in my own mind is the Dumb Dora or "woman driver" image of woman. Closely related is the dependent child, fragile flower image. As a culture we encourage women to be weak, dependent, childish, unstable, irrational, illogical, and even stupid. Jokes about the absence of female logic abound. "Woman driver" is a humorous, condescending, sometimes lovable label. Men seem to feel better, and so do women, for that matter, if the female sex isn't quite bright, or very capable, especially in "naturally" masculine pursuits like driving or fixing things, or thinking things out logically. We like women to be weak and dependent enough not to threaten what we define as the "male image."

Perhaps I'm exaggerating the way men feel about weakness and stupidity in women. Howard thinks most men don't really want a stupid and helpless wife. On the other hand he agrees that most men are threatened when women seem smarter than they, or can do things better than they can, or can do things men are "supposed" to do. And he agrees that many men like women to "sit at their feet" intellectually. Not that many men *aren't* strong and smart. They are in lots of ways. It's having to pretend that I'm not and they are even when they're not that is bad.

I grew up, and I think most women did, hearing the repeated refrain, "Don't be smarter than the boys. Don't beat a boy at anything. If you know more than he does about something, don't let on. Make him think you're interested in his superior knowledge and achievement." Enough years of that kind of brainwashing and many woman begin to feel stupid or to act stupid, or both. I know two young women, themselves students married to students, who consistently get lower grades than their husbands do *on purpose* so as not to threaten them. My own response was a less conscious one. I often felt stupid and was unable to carry on an intelligent conversation with men, even when the subject was one I knew something about. One thing that's helped is my growing sense of myself as a person, not "just a woman" who has to fit a particular image. Getting interested in a lot of different things besides home and family has helped too. I don't *feel* so dull any more. Getting with other women who are struggling with these same feelings has made a big difference. It's good to know that it's not just me, but to a large extent the way all women have been programmed. Of course some of the old feelings persist. I'm enrolled in a couple of classes this year. I notice that I feel more competent and confident in the class made up of mostly women than I do in the other class, which has more men in it!

Both Howard and I agreed that while most men don't really want a stupid woman, they also don't want a woman to be too smart or too capable outside the wifing and mothering realms. All the traditional opening of doors, the holding of chairs, the carrying of packages, are more than simply social graces. They're public ways of acknowledging man's strength against woman's weakness. At home, husbands don't routinely open doors, hold chairs, haul in the groceries, and lug the baby around! Someday when we get to an Adult-

Adult relationship between the sexes we'll open doors and carry packages for each other on the basis of individual need instead of sex.

Now I confess that there is a part of me that likes the weak, dependent, childlike, not very bright role. I remember a year or so ago my husband and I were driving along a road in England where we had rented a car for some sightseeing. Suddenly the car ahead of us lost its heavily loaded luggage carrier, which fell into the road in front of us. My husband rushed to help the other couple strain and struggle to drag the huge pack off the road. I sat in our car and watched. It wasn't until they had managed to heave it nearly to the edge that it suddenly hit me, "What am I sitting here for? How come I'm not out there helping?" My husband didn't seem to notice anything amiss in my just sitting in the car. Both of us were programmed that women are supposed to be dependent, and in such situations, fragile. And in a crisis sometimes we revert to our old programming. In some ways it's nice not to have to lift any burdens. But do I really want to be that dependent?

It's easier of course. If I'm dependent I don't have to take responsibility or risk failure. If I'm not very bright then there's no use trying to do anything significant because I wouldn't succeed anyway. On the other hand, some of the confusion I felt as a young wife and mother, and still feel at times, centered around the contradiction between the "great mother" and the "helpless little girl" expectations. I am supposed to be possessed of a kind of strength and intelligence and wisdom that can make me a refuge and strength to my husband and children. At the same time I am to be helpless and dependent when that is required by society or by the men in my life. The fact is that sometimes I am a refuge and strength, and sometimes I'm hurt and helpless and want someone to lean on. Both are me.

The two ways of being a woman—the good mother who is warm and nurturing and self-sacrificing, and the little girl who is helpless and fragile and not very bright—are both desirable and rewarded ways for a woman to behave in our culture. The one is nurturing servant for men and the other the foil for his masculinity.

But there's another way to be a woman that is undesirable, even frightening to many men and women both, and that is the image of woman as witch or shrew. Phrases like "castrating woman" and "domineering wife" describe the stereotype of the woman who fails as the mother-goddess depicted by my birthday poem. The woman who gives in to her "baser" emotions like anger and hostility, or who uses her brains too competently, is often labeled unfeminine at the least, or castrating and witchy at the most.

The other day I read a little book of quotations about women— all the words of famous men and well-known proverbs—like "Hell is paved with women's tongues." And there's the Adam and Eve story that makes Eve the villainess and the cause of all human sin.* There's some kind of fear and revulsion that Man apparently has felt over the centuries toward the strong side of Woman (which can become the shrewish side). The feeling is still there, it seems. I saw a newspaper headline the other day that said, WOMAN'S LIB CREATING GENERATION OF WEAK MEN. As though women's liberation has the power to *make* men anything, weak or otherwise. Are some women afraid of that too?

Although there's comfort in the thought that maybe men have kept women down because they're afraid of us, that's not really satisfying. For one thing, men don't need to be afraid of us. Most women have neither the intent nor the power to take over. At the same time I'm no longer content to stay down. I'm not willing to refrain from using my strong, intelligent, aggressive side because men will feel threatened. If they feel that way I hope they'll say so and then we can talk about it. How can we ever meet in the middle if we are afraid of each other? And I think I ought not to have to apologize for the occasional manifestation of my shrewish side. If that side of me shows itself too often, then I need to do something about that, not because I'm a woman, but because I'm a human being, and I want to love and be

*Although the Bible story makes it pretty clear that the serpent was the villain and that Adam was as weak as Eve in giving in to the temptation, even the organized Church has chosen to make Eve the evil one and to hold it against all women.

loved by other human beings. There *is* a witchy, shrewish, dominating side of most women (and of most men). Does that make us less female, or just more human?

Maybe when, as women, we are able to use our strong, aggressive side more directly, we won't have to use it so manipulatively and destructively. The domineering wife, the demanding and manipulating woman, will be less common. At least I find that is true of me. When I'm supposed to be a strong, competent mother and wife at home and a helpless Dumb Dora away from home, I inevitably end up behaving inappropriately. I sit helplessly in the car as I did in England, making supervising (controlling) remarks like, "Now why don't they drag it that way instead," when I might actually help do what needs doing. Or worse. I can remember times when I've verbally cut my husband down in public because I was jealous of his power and success. Now that I am freer to use my strength legitimately and openly to do my own thing I'm a lot less manipulative and shrewish.

Another reason women get witchy and shrewish is that on the whole we're taught to give and not to take. A friend of mine, who is also struggling with the second half of her life, said to me the other day, "I've spent most of my life giving, giving, giving, thinking it was naughty to take—passing to everyone else. Never take the big piece, even if nobody else does." And a young mother I know said, "I'm always doing what other people think I should do. I can't bring myself to do what *I* want. I don't think I even know what I want or how to find out. It's always been that way. I can't take. I have to give." I still find it difficult, except in a restaurant, to sit and be served. I'm mildly uncomfortable if Howard even brings me a cup of coffee, although he's often glad to do it. I'm supposed to wait on him! Some of that kind of programming is individual, of course. But the image of woman as most fulfilled when she serves is a deeply ingrained one in our culture.

To the degree that we are taught not to take, and not to be angry that we can't take, and not to use our drive and power directly, we become openly shrewish and quietly manipulating. Isn't that where phrases like "back seat driver" and "the power behind the throne" come from? How many times over the years I have struggled to figure out my husband's mood of the moment, not primarily because I cared about him, but because I wanted to decide what approach to take in order to get what I wanted. Now I try to let him know directly what my needs are, though that's still hard. He says he likes that better even though it's threatening sometimes because he then has to deal directly with my needs. But he feels less manipulated and can choose to respond honestly with his own needs and his own position. I find that when I feel free to ask for what I want or need, or even to take it, whatever the risk, I am less apt to be stealthily attacking and manipulative. Some women use physical illness or fragility or tears to manipulate men. All of us have devised a remarkable number of ways to get what we think we want. These ways are usually clear to other women but not to men. We are bound to keep many things hidden from anyone we feel has power over us.

Traditionally our culture has said that a woman's life should revolve around a man. She is to charm him, attract him sexually, bear his children, mother him, agree with him, go where he goes, accept his decisions, and appear weak so that he can feel strong. Her only power is in her ability to control him. And *that* some of us become very good at! But it doesn't make for an open and honest grownup human relationship.

In a casual conversation the other evening a number of people in the middle-years bracket were talking about how to cope with that stage of life. When my turn came I described my excitement and enthusiasm about all the things I want to do in "the next fifty years" that I hadn't even been aware of wanting to do in the first fifty. One of the men said to me, "But aren't you afraid you'll lose your femininity if you let yourself get so aggressive?" For once I kept my cool! I said that if he meant by femininity a continued willingness to stay at home, to be passive, to accept no for an answer when society says I can't do something because I'm a woman—then yes, that's the kind of femininity I hope to lose. But I don't expect to lose my interest in men or in sex, or in being warm and loving and nurturing and giving.

The "natural" aggressiveness of the mother who fends and fights for her child, like the mother bear for her cub, is both recognized and valued for women. In the context of protective mother, it's possible to speculate that a woman is most feminine when she's aggressive. Whether the maternal proclivity to fight for her children is a biological one or not, it is strong and real. Isn't it possible that that kind of aggressiveness is what some women use when they "fight" for peace, or for the poor, or for racial and sexual equality? It's the aggressiveness born of caring about other people as well as oneself and wanting to influence what happens to them. Many men have the "maternal" instinct too. Aggressiveness appears to be a human, not a sexual trait. If there are biological differences in the way males and females use their natural aggressiveness, we don't have the evidence to prove it yet.

To return to the witchy part of female aggressiveness for a minute, it seems to me that this side of women gets in the way of warm relationships with other women too. When personal status depends on being connected with the right males, women have little choice but to compete with each other for the best ones available. We often find it hard to be friends at a deep level. We get our reputation for being "catty," for example, from trying to undermine each other in male eyes. We're a threat to each other. I remember years ago, when I was still feeling strongly that a woman must fit the traditional feminine pattern, I often made remarks to my husband about a particular female friend—how domineering she was, or how aggressive—especially if she was intelligent and capable and secure and beautiful and therefore a threat to me. I was really saying, to him, "Look how lucky you are to have a submissive, feminine woman like me!" There was a time, too, in the all too recent past when I was less threatened by those female colleagues of my husband who were *not* married than by those who were. If they weren't married, at least they weren't successful as women. Or so I decided.

Not long ago we went out to dinner at a restaurant where the entertainer was an Arabian belly dancer. She was beautiful! She had a body any woman would envy and she was skilled and artistic in using it. And of course she was appropriately costumed! She moved among the tables undulating her body seductively in front of one man after another. Part of the time I watched the faces of the women in the restaurant. A few were enjoying it. Most were masked, impassive. On some faces were unmistakable expressions of contempt or hatred. I wondered how many women were thinking, "Will I lose my man because I don't have a body like that? Will he be thinking about belly dancers in bed tonight? I'd better go on a diet and get some new clothes." How sad. Going on a diet might be a good idea for many women, but not for that reason. We women can't like each other very well when we are so suspicious of each other. Any other woman is seen as a potential threat, and especially a beautiful and seductive one.

It's surprising to me how much better I like women since I no longer see them as competitors for all the men around. Now that I'm beginning to recognize that I'm not dependent on a man to define me as a person, to make me somebody, I don't have to be afraid of the power of other women. Of course I don't want to lose my husband. But if our relationship depends on my constantly striving to fit a particular image so I won't lose my man, it isn't worth it. Somehow that awareness unmasks the game we play as women and men—the game of keeping each other on our toes by subtle threats so we won't lose each other.

Women can like each other better and trust each other more when we are more sure of our worth as human beings who don't have to fit some female ideal, emotionally or bodily, in order to catch and keep a man. I didn't realize that I haven't really liked and trusted women until lately, when I've become aware of a new warmth for them. And all because of a new discovery of myself as a human being, not completely dependent on a man to make me whole.

There is a whole set of sexual traits which are also a part of the traditional image of women. They too are contradictory. On the one hand there is woman as seductress, temptress, and whore. On the other there is the idealized image of my birthday poem. That ideal woman is sexually responsive in a "nice" way, but essentially she fulfills her husband's needs unquestioningly, and finds for herself some sort of "spiritual" satisfaction in the sexual side of marriage. The soft, sweet, virgin sex object is still the male ideal of the woman to marry. The passionate and seductive temptress is the ideal "other woman."

Lately, of course, things have been changing. Increasingly the sexually ideal woman is the one who can have many orgasms and who enjoys sex as much as her partner does (without threatening his masculinity, of course, by being too demanding). There's danger here, as much as there was in the traditional image. New stereotypes are no better than old ones.

Our culture has defined sexual attractiveness in ways that place a heavy burden on all women. A young woman said to me the other day, "I get so tired of struggling to look like some contemporary version of Marilyn Monroe!" A particular combination of physical traits constitutes the traditional ideal woman: large bust, small waist, even features, no body hair except in spots, and above all, youth. Time after time in counseling sessions I talk with women, young and old, who feel inadequate because of their bust size. The woman who doesn't fit the visual image (and most of us don't) and any woman as she gets older is under tremendous pressure. Age and physical imperfection make us less "feminine." I'm aware of lots of uneasiness as I grow older. If I can't remain physically attractive, what good am I? Isn't this an almost universal feeling among women—not necessarily because they enjoy sex, but because they may not be able to hold on to a man? I know women now who are staying on the Pill long after they need to contraceptively, and long after it's medically indicated, in the hope of staving off signs of physical aging.

Single women have suffered even more than married women from the cultural insistence on marriage and motherhood as the only fully successful way to be a woman. A woman who doesn't marry often feels she is a failure as a woman, even if she is a success in other areas. If she's succeeded in a "man's world" she may be labeled masculine. Words like "old maid" and "spinster," as opposed to "bachelor" and "playboy," illustrate how we view women who either do not choose to marry or who miss out on the chance if they want it. Divorce also puts a larger stigma on women. A divorced woman is a divorcée; a divorced man is a bachelor again.

Well then, if I don't like the limits of the traditional image of woman, what do I think women should be? There shouldn't be any "should"! There cannot be—there isn't—any one ideal or image of the way a woman should be. That's exactly what the evolving identity of women—individually and collectively—is all about. The only ideal for a woman is simply for her *to be free to be whatever she can be.* A friend of mine said, "What that meant for me was being free of oughts and shoulds—free of having my actions directed by some *Women's Home Companion* image of a good wife and mother."*

This new freedom from the traditional stereotype means that as women we can be free to act and to feel without any limitation. It means we can accept and struggle with our weak and shrewish side as part of our humanness and our femaleness. It means we can feel helpless and dependent at times, and strong and independent at times without our femininity being questioned. The idealized "madonna" and the frightening "witch" images are the result of an unfortunate splitting of the loving and strong sides of women into conflicting instead of complementary facets of a woman's rich humanity. "Getting it all together" for ourselves as women, sorting out our traits and putting them together into a more integrated whole is essential for every individual woman. We must meet ourselves in the middle before we can truly meet anyone else there.

A new freedom for woman will in no way devalue her traditional roles as wife and mother. It will value them more because it will value women. But it will also mean that she can choose not to marry or not to have children without loss of status or any judgment about her femininity. She will be free to affirm her sexuality in whatever ways are satisfying to her. How passive or aggressive she is will depend on her own personality and her own needs, not on some arbitrary judgment of how women ought to be. She will be free to do as she

*Connie Leas, unpublished paper, "Issues in Woman's Liberation."

chooses both legally and culturally in her personal and occupational life.

What, then is a Woman? She's a human being, female gender. She is neither as evil nor as holy as Man would make her. She is, like Man, a blend of the good and the evil. If she's in some ways unique, if there are innate differences between the sexes in aptitudes or emotions that stem from our biological difference, we don't know yet what they are or the extent of their effect. Whatever our differences, we need to value each other equally, and that means that it must be just as exciting and satisfying in the eyes of our society to Be a Woman!, as to Be a Man!

It's exhilarating! But it's also scary. Now that I'm happier with my own vision of what a woman can be, and now that I feel freer to be me than I used to, I find myself at times more uncomfortable with myself! Some of it is dissatisfaction with the way I am now, and some of it is fear of the responsibility I have to take when I choose to use my new freedom. Although in years past I've "chafed at the bit," at least I knew what was expected of me. Now I know that there need not be any pattern that I must fit. That means choices, choices for which I must be responsible. The old programming limited me, but at least it was familiar and safe. The new way is uncharted. I will have to sink or swim on my own. Although legal and cultural limitations will remain for women for years to come, essentially I can no longer blame my husband or my children or society alone for whatever unhappiness and frustration I experience.

So what do I want to do? What is *me?* Can I affirm all that was good and satisfying in the past? Can I let go of the frustration and anger over past injustice and present limitation enough to relate to the people of both sexes who can work with me to change things for women and for society, for my daughter and for me? For my husband and my sons, too. Can I lose my dependence on what other people think enough to be able to shrug my shoulders at their labels when I step out of the traditional "feminine" role? Before I pursue what these questions will mean, I want to talk about men for a while. If women are to meet men in the middle and to love them fully, we need to try to understand them and empathize with them, and to consider what we need from them if we are to become human together.

Two / What Is a Man?

I like men. I always have. In fact, until recently, I've been much fonder of men individually and collectively than of women. But as my ideas and feelings about women and my self-awareness as a woman have changed, so have my feelings about men. Since I have been able to some degree to give up my dependence on the men in my life, especially my husband, to supply me with an identity, I have let go of much of the hurt and anger that come from feeling like an appendage. And I find companionship with a man much more fun than a sun-and-satellite relationship. I want and need men—to live and to work with, to love and to cherish and to enjoy. But my appreciation and enjoyment of them are more honest since I have felt more like a whole human being instead of an inferior one. Now I relate to men because I *choose to,* not because I *have to* in order to be a person. Oh, I haven't got rid of *all* my anger; it still comes out sometimes in explosive or witchy ways if I'm feeling put down or insecure. But as I discover better things to do with my anger and become more accepting of myself, I get less angry at men. I also have begun to feel a lot more empathy for what they're up against.

If there is a companion to "What Is a Woman," a poem called "What Is a Man?" I've never seen it. But there could be one. I've become more and more aware in recent months of the demanding and limiting qualities of the traditional definition of maleness. It is true that the demands and limits have not been so confining for men as they have been for women. The boxes they are in haven't been as small, but they definitely are boxes. The freer I begin to feel as a woman, the more I'm aware of the need for men to be free too. I often wonder now why men don't feel more anger at the way the stereotype limits them. Perhaps it's because their boxes haven't been so small and their payoffs have been more rewarding. The statement that women's liberation is really human liberation is profoundly true. Not only do both sexes need it, but we can only achieve it fully together.

There's always been a "woman problem." Newspapers, magazines, and scientific literature are full of it. But rarely is anything heard about a "man problem." Apparently there isn't one, in the same way that there's a "Negro problem" but not a "Caucasian problem." There are numerous books on the psychology of women but almost none on the psychology of men.

It has always seemed to me to be presumptuous for men to tell women what they are and what they are meant to be. So I don't want to make that mistake in reverse. I'll never know how it feels to be a man. But if we are to learn to live together differently than we have in the past, we need to do everything we can to understand each other. If I really want men to meet me in the middle, then I must struggle to understand the box men are forced into by our culture, and the load they carry as men. If I can understand to some degree, then maybe I can empathize with the way men feel in the same ways that I would like them to empathize with me. Neither sex can *fully* understand the other, I'm convinced. And I believe that the mystery is a desirable component of our celebrated uniqueness and difference. But an increased understanding of each other's humanness can bring us closer together without threatening our differentness. This chapter is my attempt as a woman to understand what men face, and to let them know what I would like from them in that context.

What *is* a man? If I again let myself drift backward to my sixteen-and-seventeen-year-old days, I see the male companion to that ideal woman as a prince charming, a knight on a white charger, handsome, strong, aggressive, tough, independent, intelligent, dominant. That man would always win, succeed, achieve! He must never fail. What a burden! The emphasis on male dominance and success means that men must dominate not only women but other men as well. Hence the cutthroat competition of the "man's world." The image of men as strong, muscular, tall, big, successful, and independent, though it is (or has been) an attractive one, is also an imprisoning one. What happens to a man who doesn't fit the image? What happens if he's small and slight? If he accepts a challenge and fails? If he loses the game or the job or the salary? What happens when, instead of conquering, he is conquered, when someone else gets the promotion? Does he feel less a man? Do other people think he's less a man? What if he happens to like opera better than football? Is he sometimes accused of being "feminine"? That's a pretty tight box for a man.

The box is constructed early, too. I remember in my elementary school days a boy who, unlike the other boys, liked to read instead of play baseball, and enjoyed folkdancing, which most boys hated (although secretly some of them liked it). He was made fun of far more cruelly than his counterpart, the tomboy, who liked baseball better than reading and boys' activities more than girls'. Boys who choose the violin or reading instead of sports are still, however subtly, made to feel they aren't measuring up to the masculine ideal. I think also of sixteen-year-old Tom, who through months of group therapy made the remark over and over again, "Why can't I just be me, instead of the way they want me to be?" He meant his parents, who wanted him to play football instead of writing poetry, to be interested in cars and girls instead of music, to work for straight As instead of being content with Bs and Cs. Be a success! Be a man!

Sometimes it seems as though we have replaced the caveman, the great hunter, with the great athlete, or the fast and daring sports car and motorcycle driver. Among the highest paid males in the nation are the famous athletes and the racing car drivers. To make it even more difficult, since World War II a high intelligence quotient has increasingly become the sign of a man. So now the ideal for a man is the I.Q. of a genius in a Mr. America body! Few men can ever approach that ideal.

The rigid image of masculinity boxes men in when it comes to feelings, too. Recently in a marriage counseling session the husband had at last allowed himself to cry real tears. His comment afterward was, "Even while the tears were coming, I could hear my mother saying to me, 'Little boys don't cry.' But I've been swallowing those tears for years. Suddenly I feel better. Why isn't it okay for men to cry?" The traditional male image has not included the freedom to feel except in a limited way. The "strong, silent type" is the ideal. Fear, pain, hurt, tenderness, gentleness, weakness, have been the province of women. The man who weeps or behaves gently is labeled "feminine" by both men and women. (It is an interesting contradiction, though, that just as women are allowed to use the "masculine" traits —aggressive protectiveness—in the mother-child relationship, so are men allowed to be tender and gentle as fathers.) The traditional image has deprived men of the option to express feelings for so long that many men have trouble letting themselves go, or teaching themselves to feel even when they have decided they want that change. The couple mentioned above came for counseling because the wife was threatening to break up their marriage. Her husband was "so cold, so distant, so busy. He really hasn't any feelings. He just doesn't care!" He really *did* care very much, but didn't know how to let himself or his wife know that. At first he was bewildered by his wife's complaints. He knew only that he wanted her and their marriage. As he began to struggle to discover whether he had any feelings, he became aware of many other childhood incidents through which he had learned to suppress all feelings signs of "weakness" and vulnerability. In the process of "getting rid of" those traits he had been forced to block out nearly *all* feeling—love, anger, and joy as well as fear and weakness. The admonitions, "Don't cry," and "Don't be afraid," and "Be a man!" also meant "Don't feel!"

Our society's demand for performance and achievement colors every facet of a man's life. Even a man who succeeds in keeping in touch with his feelings has little time for weakness or vulnerability or even for satisfying relationships and emotions. The heavy financial burden that a man must carry means he must work even harder and longer hours in the competitive world. That leaves little time and energy for loving and for living at a feeling level. Of course, it's also true that many men keep busy in order to avoid becoming aware of their feelings and the relationships that might question their success as hard-driving, aggressive males. It's safer to shut out fears of failure, loneliness, hurt, pain, dependency. It must be very lonely to be a man at times.

Many women also are threatened by a feeling man. We want men to be "gentle" but sometimes we too are afraid that means "unmasculine." How often in a group or a counseling session I have seen a woman react with anxiety when her husband or another man was finally able to admit to fear or to let the tears come. Recently one woman said to her husband after such an encounter, "I like you to have feelings but I don't want to be married to a weak man!" Some women fear a man is losing his virility if he begins to have feelings and concern for other people. Women accept the dominant values of the culture as do men. We often equate feeling with weakness— a "feminine" trait. We send our sons and husbands off into the competitive world, even to war, with little complaint. "Be a man!" We are sometimes our own worst enemies!

The performance-achievement demand also limits men's career. Even though in theory men have a wide variety of occupational choices, and although they are free to be fathers and have jobs, too, in practice men who enter artistic fields or traditionally female professions, like nursing and teaching and social work, often encounter feelings—their own and other people's—that they are not fully masculine. Some people still talk about the "demasculinization" of the American male because he is beginning to change diapers, to babysit, and to do dishes. Such nonsense! Men who enjoy doing their share of the parenting and housework are often criticized by other men, or accused of being "henpecked." One man who came with his wife for marriage counseling said he loved to cook but he didn't dare tell his fellow construction workers that.

Further, a man often feels he has failed if his wife makes more money than he does, or gains more prestige in some way. Though in a great many marriages both partners earn money, the man often feels the financial pressure in a peculiar way. Sometimes it is that she is working for fulfillment yet the main financial responsibility is still his. Sometimes he feels guilty because his wife has to work to help out.

Men have a difficult time if they want to change jobs in middle life. Most boys are pressured to make occupational choices very early in life, often before they really have a chance to know where their interests and resources lie. Then they are saddled with financial responsibility which makes any change difficult if they find later on that they've made a mistake. If a man decides he needs to do something new with his life, the option is open (that is, he can retain his masculinity) only if he can continue to support his family and be a financial success. I remember when Howard decided he would like to get another degree, for he had developed new interests. But by then he had a growing family and he couldn't do it. I felt guilty about that. But struggle as we might, we couldn't think of a solution. I had to take care of the children and he had to earn the money! Other options didn't occur to us then.

Thus we box men in pretty tightly and pretty early and force them down a particular path in the same way we do women. Women have had but one fully acceptable occupational choice while men have had many. But men are limited too, in when and where and how they can pursue their choices and still be men. Many younger men these days feel the heavy hand of society's expectations that they shape up as males, which translated means: decide on a lifetime career and commit yourself to earning a living in it.

Our cultural stereotype does something else to men that is represented by the domineering wife–henpecked husband syndrome, a dehumanizing one for both partners. For whatever reasons it develops—and I come across many in counseling—at the root of it there always seems to be some fear of the woman on the man's part. Even when a man is highly successful in the outside world, he is often a Caspar Milquetoast or a Dagwood Bumstead at home. We make fun of men in the comics and on television, in books and movies, for this apparent weakness in the face of women. The situation is often blamed on the domineering wife (who took over from a manipulative mother). She shouldn't try to be the boss because it makes a man feel less masculine. But how is it that women can take over so easily if men are so strong? Is it possible for a man really to be "head of the house" only if a woman is willing to "stay in her place"? Are we playing the game that says men are weak and women are strong and the rules are that women must pretend to be weak so that men can be strong? And that the domineering wife and henpecked husband are not playing by the rules?

Partly, but I think there's more to it than that. There is a good deal of evidence that over the centuries men *have* feared women. That's something I have trouble understanding in any really personal way. I've always been somewhat afraid of men, and I can't imagine their being afraid of me. Psychoanalyst Karen Horney, one authority on the male fear of the female, remarks on the jealousy and fear in men of the female power of creation.* It is the woman who menstruates and bears the child, and that's pretty mysterious. Besides, men were all once little boys raised by big mothers—and mothers actually are pretty powerful creatures to small boys (girls, too). Wherever these fears are rooted—in the little boy that is in every man, in the lack of understanding about the female biological function from the dawn of humanity—the fear seems to be there in many men. The remark of Cato the Elder in 195 B.C. echoes what lots of men seem to be feeling even now: "Suffer women once to arrive at an equality with you, and they will from that moment become your superiors." Does that follow? I don't think so. Our mistake, I believe, has been in assuming that the patriarchal myth—man as the master whom woman must obey—is the only successful one for human beings. In fact, the evidence is that the most mutually satisfying female-male relationships are those in which who is the "head of the house" is not an issue. Men and women both are strong—and weak. But we keep right on playing the "I'll be weak so you can be strong" game. Some men and women choose to play it in reverse, and then we have the henpecked husband and the domineering wife. There are other alternatives.

*Karen Horney, *Feminine Psychology* (New York: W. W. Norton, 1967).

When Howard and I began to change our relationship, he did feel threatened by my increasing independence and my unwillingness to play the old one up–one down games. He says he didn't feel henpecked, just deprived. But most of the things I was depriving him of were the mothering things—not being there to fix his lunch, not being available every time he needed or wanted me. Fortunately he often was able to recognize the hurt little boy in himself. And of course it *is* nice to be waited on. But my being less available for those functions didn't mean I was taking over or becoming a domineering wife, or wanting to. Neither did my wanting to share the satisfactions of the "male world."

Some of the male fear of women must stem from their experience of the shrewish and manipulative side of woman. Women *do* try to control men when they feel they can't get what they need any other way. They are less apt to try if they have legitimate ways to use their strength. So I hope that men can learn to deal with their little boy fears and won't continue to feel they have to keep women in their places so they won't usurp the power. Most women don't want to do that. And even if they do, men aren't that weak! I can't dominate a man unless he lets me.

Another thing often happens to men in our patriarchal system. They are too often essentially distant figures to their children. It is mother, not father, who wields the influence and power at home. Oh, she may often say, "Wait till I tell your father," or "Sh! Here comes your father." But frequently she is only using him to maintain her own power while he remains a shadowy figure in the background —no model of masculinity for either his sons or his daughters who grow up to perpetuate the pattern.

In a counseling session one woman told me of her childhood memories of her clergyman father, a highly respected and successful man in his profession. He did most of his work at home in a study with the door closed. She remembers her awe and fear of that closed door and her mother's constant admonitions to the children not to go in, not to make noise. As she looks back now, she's aware of her father as someone she never knew, someone who was endowed with power and influence at home by her mother, who made him seem important to his children, even though he had little to do with them. Her mother was literally the "power behind the throne."

There is the opposite style for men too. Some husbands and fathers become tyrants both physically and emotionally. Such men insist on maintaining a rigid authoritarianism at home, demanding absolute obedience from wife and children. Sometimes these are men who have not succeeded in their jobs and so must prove their masculinity at home. They may be men who need to be in charge everywhere. They may be highly "successful" men. Either way they often have cowering wives who indulge the children. They themselves often push their children, especially their sons, into the performance-achievement box with a vengeance. In my experience as a counselor I see the sons become like their fathers if they can, or strike back with drugs or delinquency or suicide if they can't.

I'm aware that I've been describing three male extremes—the henpecked husband, the distant husband and father, the authoritarian. Some men do fit one or the other of these extremes. But most men find themselves struggling between them, caught in the dilemma of how to be a human being and still be a man. If you're a father, maybe you can see yourself fitting into one or more of those categories some of the time.

The pressure we have put on men in the area of sexuality is a demanding one too. Although men have been traditionally freer, under the double standard, to enjoy sex in a variety of ways not open to women, the demand and performance quality of the acceptable male role is high. I worked some time ago with a group of newly married couples who were talking over some of their feelings and concerns about the expectations they had of themselves sexually. One young man described his youthful anxiety about whether he would be able to "perform" adequately enough to keep a woman happy. Would he be able to live up to the image of the male as always interested in sex, always ready, and always successful? What would happen if he should be tired, or depressed, or anxious, and couldn't "perform"? Wouldn't his wife see him as less of a man, perhaps even stop loving him? Most of the women present had assumed that men have few if any doubts about sex. It came as a surprise to hear almost all the other men resonate to one man's worries.

It seems to me that men would be much freer if they were released from the "demand" quality of sexuality and the emphasis on performance. Such release would free both men and women sexually. If men were not always required to perform sexually, they wouldn't need to see women mainly as sex objects; the playboy image implies a man constantly alert and at the ready. And it is necessary for a man to keep a woman weak and objectified sexually only if he is unsure of his own sexual competence. A woman must be a passive sex object only if she is afraid her man isn't really strong and she could easily threaten him. Loosening the bonds of what *must* happen sexually if a man is to be a man would help free all of us.

One of the ways that the rigid masculine image has limited men is in their dress. I'm glad to see that changing. New styles and bright colors for men are a pleasure to behold. This morning I took the car in for a checkup. A male customer was there for the same reason. He caught my eye and I liked what I saw. He had on powder blue slacks with belt to match, a blue and white striped shirt and blue tie. Although these colors are more common among men now, they still are unusual enough to command my attention. And I was aware of my pleasure, my desire to look him up and down in much the same way a man does a woman, I suppose. I'm glad men are getting away from the drab, gray flannel suit image.

The physical requirements for men, though less demanding than those for women, are nonetheless real. The small men, the less hairy men, are often suspect as males. Men also feel the loss of sexual attractiveness with increasing age—baldness, flabbiness, loss of physical stamina. Maybe that's why so many men try to prove their masculinity with other women.

The masculinity trap, then, is constructed with rigid requirements for masculinity in much the same way that women are boxed in by their limited programming. Toughness, drive, hostile aggression, achievement at any cost, the strong silent image, emotional control, self-sufficiency, unyieldingness, independence, rationality, size, are some of the materials with which the trap is built. Too many men still grow up believing that they must deny their soft, tender, nurturing side for fear they will be labeled weak and feminine. Loss of a job, failure to be promoted, to make money, to provide material things for his family—all can be devastating for a man because these are the traditional marks of success. The tooth and claw success story dehumanizes the man who succeeds as well as the man who fails. Men who succeed have to tramp on other people—men and women —to get there. And the rat race appears to lower life expectancy for men dramatically. Would men be healthier, and more equal to women in life expectancy, if they didn't have to work so hard, compete so intensely, hold in their feelings so tightly, worry so much about success? How good it would be if as men and women we could share the burdens of earning a living as well as those of domesticity.

Although I don't think I've ever wanted actually to *be* a man, I have often wondered what it *feels* like to be one. Some parts I think I would like—the power, the status, the sexual freedom and easier sexual satisfaction, the open opportunities for achievement in a variety of areas, the being waited on, having meals set in front of me, not having to think about the laundry, or the floor wax, for example. But then I also wonder what it would be like to be always under the pressure of achievement, pressure to bring in lots of money, pressure to succeed. When performance and achievement and creativity, other than biological or domestic, are demanded of me—even though I'm now choosing to do things that bring those demands— I get uneasy and afraid. I wouldn't like having the *whole* financial burden of a family, feeling the pressure to succeed because someone else's identity depended on my success, or not being able to show any real feelings of pain or to cry real tears. And I wouldn't like not having time and intimacy with my children.

I'm aware that not all men feel this much pressure in being a man. Some simply don't let themselves become aware of it. Some, like some women, really are free. These are the self-actualizing people who are not bound by society's rigid definitions of masculinity and femininity. Still, I have the feeling that most men, like most women, are to a greater or less degree boxed in by the rules, and to that extent are unable to become fully human. I hope that you who are men won't feel that what follows is a long list of a woman's demands. It isn't meant to be that at all. It is meant to be an affirmation of the changes that are happening in men. Men are sometimes heard to ask, often in an exasperated tone, "What does a woman want, anyway?" Well, here is what turns one woman on:

I do like some of the same things I used to admire—strength, courage, and drive to succeed. But now I like it best when these qualities are tempered with others. I like a man who values relationships as much as he does monetary or prestigious success in society. It feels good to me when Howard says, "I don't like this rat race I'm in. I need more time with you!" I like it when he wants to take time to cultivate relationships with his wife and family and friends.

I like men who are willing to take their share of the routine of everyday living, who aren't so hung up on whether or not they are masculine that they can't put their hands in the dishwater or cook a meal.

I like a man who is in touch with his feelings and willing to share them, the whole range of them—joy, passion, playfulness, tenderness, pleasure, apathy, sadness, ambition, fear, despair. I like a man who can cry.

Some men have a concern for nurturing the world, for preserving life, not just for dominating or conquering it. I want them to know that to me they seem stronger, not weaker, when they feel like that.

I like a man who is willing to relate to me as an equal, who doesn't need to define the limits of what I can do and feel and still be a woman. I like a man who doesn't have to make cutting remarks about "a woman's place" whenever the subject of women comes up. Sometimes a man says to me, "I never knew women really feel so hurt or so put down." I like a man who can recognize my hurt and his own threatened feelings and accept the need for change anyway. Such men can understand my need for equality without feeling I'm trying to take over, to dominate them, to usurp power. I like men who are willing to share life with women on an equal plane rather than on a one up–one down basis—with men always up.

I like a man who respects my independence without his masculinity being threatened by my wanting to share some of the financial burden and the satisfactions of achieving something in the outside world. I like a man who is able to accept and affirm my strong, aggressive, ambitious, achieving side, who doesn't need me to be weak and stupid in order for him to feel masculine. I like a man who isn't threatened by my negative feelings, especially anger. He doesn't have to like them! It's okay with me if he gets angry, too!

I like men who appreciate our physical and biological differences and respect both. I like my husband to enjoy sex, and to be able to accept his own strengths and vulnerabilities and mine too. I'm glad he is secure enough in himself not to need to be sexually successful a hundred percent of the time. I like him to be able to enjoy a whole range of sexual experiences with me without being hung up on what's acceptable for a man or a woman and what isn't.

I like it when men appreciate my body as different from theirs, and like me to appreciate their bodies as well. I like a man who affirms my sexuality, not as an object, but as an intelligent human being who has brains as well as legs and breasts—in the same way that I can be attracted to a man physically but not therefore discount his intelligence and capabilities.

I like a man who is willing to let me get older without rejecting me sexually and physically, and who can cope with his own feelings about getting older without being so threatened that he has to "prove himself" with younger women—or many women. I like a man who can, to some degree, see himself as a worthwhile human being at any stage of life, and is willing to see me that way too. I like a man who can relate to a woman first as another human being and then as a woman. I like a man who likes these same qualities in a woman.

That's a pretty big order. But all I'm really saying is that I want men to be human and to treat me as human. And I think women have as much responsibility for changing relationships between the sexes as men do.

I'm well aware that in some ways such relationships are as yet pretty unrealistic in light of the tenacious quality of traditional male-female roles. But I've also been surprised and gratified in recent months to find that there are lots of men who do relate to women this way or are willing to learn. And there have always been some men who didn't accept the stereotypes in the first place. Still, I don't think there's any man, however liberated, who if he is honest with himself, isn't aware of being mildly to severely threatened at times by changing roles and identities. (I don't think I know any women who aren't threatened either.) But a remarkable number of men are beginning to be able to hear what more and more women are saying about the humanizing ways they want to be treated, and are also becoming aware of how the male role definitions have deprived men of the fullness of life.

I wonder whether men as a group will sooner or later find out that they're angry too, not so much at women's growing freedom as at the centuries–old prison they've kept themselves in, partly from the need to keep woman in her place. The male position of privilege is also a prison. It's my experience that as men are discovering this, they begin to do things to change their side of relationships.

Maybe what we have done with our tight male and female boxes has been even harder on men than on women. The constant pressure to keep the superior position must explain much male fear and defensiveness and false confidence. The awareness, both conscious and unconscious, that your strength is partly based on someone else's weakness, must be a heavy burden to bear.

What then, is a man? He's a human being, male gender. Like a woman, he's a combination of weakness and strength, good and evil. Whatever his innate biological and temperamental endowment, he needs to be free to be whatever he can be, to fulfill his potential in whatever ways he finds creative and satisfying, so long as they are not destructive to himself or others.

This new masculinity is beginning to emerge in some men as the new femininity is emerging in some women. The gains for men are a new freedom to feel and a relaxation of the terrible burden of performance, achievement, and success. And that inevitably means new and more satisfying relationships with women and with other men too. I've heard a couple of men say that as they let down some of their defenses about what it means to be masculine, they have been able to talk to other men in a more human way. They lose some of the need to pretend to each other that they always feel successful. For Howard and me, our joint efforts to get out of our respective masculine and feminine boxes is a continuing challenge, and has many rewards in more intimacy and openness and excitement between us.

Three / Equal though Different

Definitions of femininity and masculinity are changing. However we feel about it, the tide has turned. We are moving toward the time when distinguishing the sexes on the basis of what we do, how we feel, and how we look will have little importance. Women are now beginning to value themselves more and to insist on being valued equally by men and by society. That means that the "weaker sex," the "second sex," the "inferior sex," are phrases which will disappear from the language.

Some people are alarmed by the thought of equality between the sexes. It does mean change, and change is always somewhat frightening. Certainly it means that both sexes will have to give up some things. Men will have to give up dependence on women as an automatic servant class and will have to move over to make room for women in public life. Women will have to give up their helplessness and dependence for identity on men.

For me, of course, there seems nothing to lose, except that dependency and a false sense of security, of being taken care of. Life seems open and challenging and exciting, and all I want is more time. It's harder, I think, for men to feel that there are gains for them when women start to change. The losses seem more obvious and more painful. Men are used to women being a certain way, staying in a certain place, letting men's interests come first, letting men have their own way. Most men probably won't move over without a push from women. Being on top, though burdensome, has its satisfactions.

Our experience is, though, that the alarm is all out of proportion to the danger. Howard and I have found that the losses are not so great as the gains for both of us in this new style of relating. Both of us are better able to escape the prisons of "ought" and "should" that we have been in for so long. We can be freer to live more creative and satisfying lives, individually and together. We can enjoy each other more and be more supportive of each other when we can let down our defenses and be human beings first.

As women and men we are in this thing of being alive together. Someone has said that (except for superficial things like skin color) blacks and whites are the same but equal while men and women are different but equal. As women and men we share intricately inter-woven lives. We live in the same houses, raise the same children, work in the same offices and schools and industries, love and hate and want and need each other every day of our lives. We *must* find ways of valuing and affirming each other and what goes on between us. For we need each other so much—as human beings, as men and women. We have so much to give to and get from each other.

For centuries, all over the world, the "battle of the sexes" has revolved around the issues of dominance and submission, weakness and strength. What many women are now asking for is a genuine *interdependence,* which is what I mean by the word "equality." It is a sharing of the load, of the leadership, of the burdens and the joys of being human. It means being mutually affirming of each other's full humanness. It means hanging loose about sex roles—what Mas-low describes as a "desexualizing of the statuses of strength and weakness, and of leadership so that either man or woman can be, without anxiety and without degradation, either weak or strong, as the situation demands. Either must be capable of both leadership and surrender."*

The issue in equality of the sexes is not that women must become "like men" or that men must become "like women," particularly not in imitating the other's worst qualities! There is nothing to be gained if women going into politics become warlike or men moving into relationships become weak or dependent. Equality doesn't mean that

*Abraham Maslow, *The Farther Reaches of Human Nature* (New York: Viking Press, 1971), p. 367.

we are to give up whatever turns out to be our uniqueness as males and females either. We will always be anatomically different. A new word has appeared in the language to describe what people fear: unisex. Many are afraid that the long-celebrated "difference" will disappear. Not a chance!

We're confused; most of us are so used to external differences that we find it hard to imagine how we will be able to remain different if we eliminate rigid female and male role and behavior differences. It's true that lately the changes in dress and hair length among both sexes, especially the youth, have let down some of the traditional barriers to how men and women can and cannot look. So both sexes are experimenting with new styles in the same way that both sexes of all ages are experimenting with new occupations. When the role divisions get blurred in one area, they are inclined to get blurred in another, too. The sort of "unisex" look among some adolescent boys and girls seems to me to reflect both a healthy experimentation with new ways of being human, and their own particular stage of identity development. They are struggling with who they are, which includes the struggle with sexual identity. It is of interest that as boys' hair has grown long, girls' hair has grown even longer.*

Several weeks ago in the grocery store I observed the following interchange: A middle-aged man, in a "gray flannel suit" was pushing a cart along the aisle, apparently picking up a few groceries on the way home from work. He approached from behind a youth with blond hair to the shoulders, wearing jeans and an old white dress shirt. He watched intently until the youth turned around, whereupon he said with an edge of anger in his voice, "I couldn't tell whether you were a boy or a girl." To which the girl replied, "That's your problem, not mine." She was right, of course. But it is a shock when you've spent fifty years getting used to boys with short hair and blue jeans and girls with long hair and dresses to see them not worrying much about surface appearances. They can't always recognize each

---

*I'm not overlooking the fact that *some* young people are reflecting serious identity and self-esteem problems in the way they dress and behave.

other from behind either but it doesn't seem to bother them. Styles in dress do not make the woman or man, contrary to long-standing opinion.

Styles of behavior sometimes seem more crucial, but do we really know that a wonan is less feminine just because she's a telephone linewoman? Or a man is less masculine because he stays home to do the laundry? Styles of masculinity and femininity have always been in flux. "In the 16th century a gentleman was 'gentle.' He played the lute and sang; he was appalled if he had a callous on his hand."* But his masculinity was not in question. My own experience, among both my friends and my clients, is that men who are the most sure of their masculinity have little trouble enjoying their gentle sides and in being nurturing and caring; women who are sure of their femininity find it less difficult to do things not ordinarily approved for women. Conversely, people who are most rigid in the ways they stick to the sexual sterotypes are most anxious about their sexuality. There is evidence that relaxing the rules about femininity and masculinity—blurring the stereotypes—allows people to enjoy their own sexuality and each other more fully.

I believe that as females and males, we enjoy our "difference" enough that we will always find ways to enhance it, to make ourselves attractive to each other. The different-but-equal philosophy simply says that where merit and opportunity are concerned a meeting in the middle is the only way we can be fully human together. It will take simultaneous changes among both women and men. It may be difficult, threatening, and slow as well as challenging and exciting. But it appears increasingly inevitable.

There's a system called Transactional Analysis** that I've found

---

*Faubion Bowers, "The Sexes: Getting it all Together," *Saturday Review,* (June 8, 1971), p. 16.

**I refer to Eric Berne's model of personality interaction: Each of us has three parts, or sides, to her or his personality—the Parent side, the Adult side, the Child side. The Parent side is nurturing or critical or both; the Child side is fun-loving or rebellious, or both. It is the feeling side. The Adult side makes the realistic decisions that get us where we want to go. We act according to which side is "turned on" at the moment. We enter into "transactions" or interactions with each other according to which side helpful in understanding what goes on between women and men. Our culture says, generally, that men are one-up and women are one-down. Thus the strong or one-up sex takes the Parent role and the weak or one-down sex takes the Child role. Between individual men and women these roles are often reversible, and we take turns being Parent and Child. When, in the early days of our marriage, I whisked the magazine under the pillow at my husband's approach, I was playing guilty Child. Since he probably would have been disapproving if he caught me reading a magazine instead of fixing dinner, he would have been playing critical Parent. We all relate to each other that way some of the time. All of us need to be dependent sometimes. When Howard is sick or down, I am glad to mother him (unless I'm also sick and down). He's willing to do the same for me. And of course Parent-Child relationships are appropriate between parents and children. Unfortunately, at home the woman often becomes Parent and the man takes the Child role, with the woman attempting to supply all the man's desires including his insatiable, neurotic needs. Often too, she becomes witchy Parent, as her anger comes out in controlling and demanding ways.

When most of our communication with each other as individual men and women and as sexes is some form of Parent-Child interaction, we cannot be equal either in value or in opportunity. We manipulate each other in "I-it" relating. Unfortunately, much of our individual and collective life is based on Parent-Child ways of relating. We would like each other better as persons, female and male, and discover our own and each others' strengths more easily if we could reach out to each other as equal partners and face together the full range of pain and joy in being human. That requires an Adult-Adult relationship, both individually and collectively.

In the early years of our marriage, Howard and I had mostly a sun and satellite, or Parent and Child, relationship. He was the busy,

---

of us is in control or which side is "turned on" by the other person. Thus if someone says to me, "You're stupid!" his Parent is turned on. I may reply either, "I am not!" (defensive Child) or "Poor little me!" (helpless Child) or, if I could get my Adult side functioning, "What is your evidence?"

achieving one; I was the grateful, dependent one. Most of my feeling of being important, came from being married to him, reflected glory like the satellite. The other side of the coin was that I served as Parent and he became indulged Child at home. I fed him and took care of his clothes, entertained when he needed it, and took care of the children. In many ways this was satisfying for both of us. And we did feel that we were doing what was "right." But in both of us, though we were unaware of it, was the underlying guilt and anger. Much of the guilt and anger and the distance between us were results of the basic unfairness of the arrangement for both of us, especially for me. The fact is that our roles were to a large degree culturally determined for us. They were not our own free choices. I'm aware now that I felt deprived and resentful, and therefore became manipulative and controlling. He now says that he felt guilty because somewhere deep down he knew he was exploiting me. He also felt deprived of close relationships with his children. And he and I could not be truly intimate in that kind of relationship.

I'm not suggesting that I think it was chiefly what we *did* that caused the dissatisfaction. I think it was the way we valued each other and ourselves, and the way we were valued by society. There is no doubt in my mind that couples can successfully follow a pattern similar to our early life style and be "equal." But only if they make conscious choices to do it that way, and truly like their choices. And only if they both find real rewards in their choices and are able to share the unrewarding parts. Also, society must value the contribution of one as highly as that of the other. It won't work if mothering and housekeeping continue to have low status, and women are automatically programmed into those roles exclusively. It won't work if it is automatically assumed that the man always will have both the full burden of financial responsibility and the rewards and success of higher status.

In some ways it's a difficult and painful thing to equalize a relationship which has been chiefly Parent-Child or sun-satellite for many years. When I first started not being home for lunch every day, Howard felt deprived. And I found it difficult to recognize that it was as much my responsibility as his to keep gas in the car. Those are just the little things, the tip of the iceberg. Many things are harder than the old way because we have to plan and negotiate our differences and argue at times about whose responsibility is what. But the gains are big. Our change was the kind we needed. Your changes may be very different. There must be as many successful ways to become human together as there are people. The crucial issue is that we are valued fully by society and that we value ourselves and each other equally.

Sad to say, the Parent-Child, male-female ways of relating are perpetuated by the laws of our land (again with women usually one down), and with dehumanizing effects on both sexes. In our safety deposit box at the bank rests a document given to me by my husband last Christmas. Here's how the gift came about: Some weeks before Christmas a story appeared in the paper about the Women's Equalization Committee which was organizing to fight legal discrimination against women in California. "Give your wife equality for Christmas!" invited the headline. The gift would be in the form of a legal document which when signed by a husband would give his wife "a voice and power equal to mine in the choice and mode of our living" and equal power in the management and control of community property. When I saw the article I said to my husband half facetiously, half seriously, "Now, *there's* what you can give me for Christmas!" And half jokingly and half seriously he did!

The law in California says that a husband may choose "any reasonable place or mode of living, and the wife must conform thereto." Interests of husband and wife in community property are "present, existing, and equal," *but* "under the management and control of the husband." Now how can that be equal? Thus the document. When I looked at it I was aware of some anger that my rights have to be given to me by my husband, and guilt that I do not feel grateful for being married to a man who is willing to be so good to me! Actually, I *do* feel glad to be married to a fair-minded man, but I don't think I ought to *have* to feel grateful for a right which is morally already mine as a human being!

A couple of weeks after Christmas, Howard asked me if I wanted to have the document notarized. I had mixed feelings about the whole thing. I want to be legally free and equal. But somehow the document itself, the public notarizing, seemed just too insulting—like the master freeing the slave. Howard felt caught in that dilemma too. If he *didn't* give me such a document, then we were legally bound by an unjust law. If he *did* give it to me, we were cooperating with an unjust system that lets one person give (or withhold from) another the freedom which is rightfully hers. Well, we didn't get it notarized. I just couldn't bring myself to do it! So there it sits in the safety deposit box, in case my husband should ever turn into a tyrant and I should need it.

Because, you see, it isn't as though the question raised by my document is likely to be a practical one for me. Howard wouldn't do what the law gives him the power to do—make unilateral decisions about where we should move or about how our property should be managed. It's the principle of the thing! And it's more than the principle of the thing for many people. Many men like the legal one-up position. Too many women are victimized when the law supports their husbands' unreasonable and unfair demands. On the other hand, not all women want to share the load of being equally responsible for decision-making. They are willing to play the "I'm not really very bright about business matters" game in order to be taken care of. Many couples would rather avoid the hassle and the pain of the kind of communication it would require for them to compromise fairly their different wants and needs. Thus as men and women we cooperate with a law like the one above. Certainly there's nothing wrong with a division of labor. But that isn't the issue here. The issue is the genuine equality of rights before the law.

Here's where all women have legitimate reason for anger. Sometimes our anger carries us away and we attack men inappropriately. That's when it sounds like we're trying to take over. I myself had to rewrite this section four times before I could get the anger toned down! And even now I'm sure you can still feel it.

The lethal game of "wise father–helpless little girl" has many social and legal consequences. How does it make you feel to realize that the median salary for working women (in 1970) is only slightly over half that for men? Did you know that although the total number of women working outside the home has increased (nine out of ten work for some period of their lives; six out of ten work outside the home full time, some of them for thirty years), the percentage of women in professional work has steadily *decreased* sinced 1940? Are you aware that in most states if you are a woman you would have trouble establishing credit in your own name, no matter how much money you make? Did you know that *most* divorced women with children are incapable (that is, they haven't the education or training) of making an adequate living even if they can find care for their children, and that *most* child support payments are either inadequate or nonexistent?

The law reinforces and is reinforced by the Parent-Child game that keeps one sex weaker both in rights and in feeling. For it is true that women have been told for so long that they are inferior they have come to believe it themselves. That means that only the most self-assured women push for equal pay, a chance to advance at the same rate as men, and the opportunity to enter traditionally male occupations. Only the most self-assured are willing to fight for their rights in marriage and divorce. And even such independent women often fail because the law and the cultural mystique do not back them up. Frequently, if they do succeed, they incur the stigma of the "unfeminine" label.

To be fair we must also acknowledge that some laws discriminate against men, particularly the child custody and alimony laws and the draft law. There is no doubt that both women and men have a right to be angry. Change in the unjust laws is a first and essential step toward the goal of treating all persons equally in practice. And that has already begun to happen. Equal pay for equal work is now federal law. The Equal Rights Amendment already passed by Congress makes illegal all discrimination according to sex, including that which discriminates against men. Women are beginning to be heard and heeded, which is encouraging. But it is slow work. The obvious fact is that simply passing laws does not end discrimination. The Blacks and Chicanos are well aware of that, and so are women who still get paid less for the same work, even though that's now against the law. The burden of proof is still with the victim and only the strongest will choose to fight. But legally the die is cast and equality will come.

Role stereotypes are even more difficult to get rid of than are discriminatory laws. Even *I* found myself uncomfortable when I saw the women in Russia working right along with the men on heavy construction projects. And I never did get used to men holding hands in India. But in neither place did I see any evidence that women and men like each other less, simply because they define behaviors differently.

Of course there are many subtle ways, too, in which women are made to feel inferior. One of these is our language, which uses "man" and "mankind" and the masculine pronouns exclusively when referring to both sexes. At first such considerations seem petty. But consider the unconscious imprinting that is begun at birth for little girls when they hear themselves consistently left out of the language. Then it seems less petty. Phrases like "man and wife" (never "woman and husband"), "man and woman," or "male and female," never the reverse, the use of "he" whenever only one man is present in a group of women—all seem to suggest the assumption that men come first, and are more important.

I was thinking the other day about the Declaration of Independence: ". . . all men are created equal." But, you say, that means women, too? It doesn't though, as becomes obvious in any discussion of legal and social rights. And the language is powerful. It's both cause and effect. How do you like: "We hold these truths to be self-evident, that all women are created equal. . . ." We do need some changes in the way we use the language, either some new words or more inclusive ways of using the old ones or both. Maybe you've noticed that I've been saying "women and men" as often as "men and women," and using both "he" and "she" when speaking generically.

One thing that's helped me in this whole matter of language is adopting the title Ms. instead of Mrs. Men are not designated by marital status and I don't believe that women should be valued according to that standard either. At first Ms. was hard on Howard. He felt I was rejecting both him and our marriage when I began feeling that I didn't want to be labeled married, despite the fact that I like both him and marriage most of the time. He's accepted Ms. now, even likes it, he says. Many women still like the traditional titles, and they should keep them if they do. Men should have married and unmarried titles too if they want them. But women should not be required to designate their marital status any more than men should. The day will come eventually when words and labels won't matter. But until that time, some kind of self-conscious change is necessary to hasten the raising of consciousness on the issue. Since I've become aware of my own need to be a human being in my own right, with an identity that doesn't depend on my husband, these things have become important. Recently my husband has begun addressing letters to me, when we are apart, with Ms. I'm glad he sees me as a person, and not as an extension of himself, as "just his wife." Both the law and the language perpetuate the "woman-as-property" syndrome.

Not all women feel the issues of equality and inferiority so strongly. Some women become strong and independent and able to live their lives fully in spite of the cultural limitations. Individuals, both female and male, develop differently according to their own childhood and adolescent experience, as well as according to cultural requirements. The fact remains, though, that the lower status of women has increased and complicated self-esteem and identity problems in most women. It is dramatically illustrated by women everywhere these days who suddenly experience the "click"—the sudden awareness that they have been "kept in their places," that they are angry about it, and that they don't intend to put up with it any more. It is illustrated by the growing number of women who are becoming aware of dissatisfaction. Some of them join a women's consciousness-raising group. Often they start out with a "Women, ugh!" feeling and come away saying, "Why it isn't just my problem like I always thought it was! We *all* feel that anger and guilt and resentment!" Women who have little in common in other ways, who probably would never be particular friends, feel pulled together in a kind of sisterhood that transcends other differences. And it has a power, too, that shows in the many changes that are already happening for women everywhere.

"Sisterhood" and "brotherhood" are good. But we must not allow those bonds to polarize us as sexes, to keep us from becoming human together. We must struggle to understand each other and to empathize with each other in order to achieve the kind of equality we are talking about. Some time, try a fantasy with yourself. Close your eyes. Imagine that you wake up one morning and find that you have become a person of the other sex. How does it feel as you lie there in bed discovering the change? Get up and look in the mirror. What's your reaction? Take yourself through a day in the body of the other sex. What does it feel like? Now go back to bed and to sleep, in your fantasy, and imagine you wake up the next day with your own body. Leave the fantasy and think about it. Was it hard to get into the body of the other sex? What sort of encounter was it?

People have varied experiences when they try that fantasy. One young woman who is a doctor found that in her fantasy as a male doctor she was treated with much more respect by the nurses and as an equal by the other male doctors. Another woman felt the pressure of being a man in her fantasy. It was like a weight, the financial responsibility for a family; she never was able to leave the mirror in her fantasy. One woman felt angry when she woke up next day in her own body. She had felt the freedom of being a man. A man had the experience of feeling trapped when he found himself in a female body. He couldn't do what he wanted to do. Another man could not get himself through a day in his new female body because he felt he wouldn't be accepted by the people in his world.

Experiences like these, if we are willing to risk them, help us to get in touch with our feelings about ourselves and each other. They can help us to understand and appreciate each other more. They can help us recognize and burst out of the boxes we keep ourselves and each other in. Talking together, refusing to put each other down, insisting on equal treatment under the law, raising our individual and collective consciousness about the human pain caused by the current system, can hurry us along to the time when we affirm the right each individual has to be what she or he can be.

Between women and men, things can never be the same again. The old dominance-submission pattern is on the way out. What will replace it? For the first time in history we have the opportunity to consciously develop new ways of relating between the sexes. If we're willing to do that—to live intentional lives as men and women —it may be that together we will discover ways to make it possible for every individual to become the fuller person that she or he can become. "Therefore it is not so much competitiveness or aggressiveness or submission or exploitation of either sex by the other that is at issue, as the opportunities each one of us, being human, can find to enjoy and be enjoyed by, help and be helped by, stimulate and be stimulated by members of the sex that is not ours, as well as the one that is."*

The next chapters will explore some of these opportunities that each one of us has to learn to live together both for our own individual fulfillment and for the survival and fulfillment of humanity.

*Mary Calderone, *Life,* September 4, 1970, p. 24.

Four / Liberated Marriage

What happens when a husband and wife try to meet in the middle —when two people who are determined to be "free and equal" try to live together in a relationship as intimate as marriage? Howard and I have been finding out about that for a few years now. Sometimes it's rough going. Often the fur flies! There *are* new tensions and problems. But at the same time, our friendship has grown, our love has deepened, and we find our marriage more exciting than it used to be. It's been an evolving process with new struggles, new roles, and new stages of getting used to each other, with each step toward a more mutual relationship. We accepted the principle years ago that freedom and equality are desirable in marriage; the challenge has been to find out what that means and then to live it out on a day-to-day basis in a society that does not really support the idea. How does a lofty principle like equality in marriage work on Monday morning and Saturday night and Thursday at five o'clock? How does it work when our needs conflict? What are the rewards and are they worth it?

For us the satisfactions have far outweighed the headaches in changing from a marriage in which Howard's needs and career plans came first most of the time to one in which our needs have equal consideration. Most obvious has been the change that has taken place in me—the awakening that I have already described. Howard says that for him the change has meant that he has a more interesting and alive person to live with.

The more we've been able to experience real equality in our relationship the more we've been able to enjoy "creative conversation" about everything from home and family to politics and religion and our respective professional interests. We even enjoy "creative argument" sometimes! Friendly arguments didn't used to be possible because of our mutual defensiveness. Now Howard has less need to be always the smart one and the right one, and I have more confidence in myself and less need to see him that way. So we can talk as two human beings instead of as paper dolls labeled "wife" and "husband."

We've discovered that there's so much we don't know about each other. I'm learning how he feels about being a man. He's learning how I feel about being a woman. We've begun to share our feelings about getting older. That means that we've lowered our defenses and become more willing to trust each other with what we really are and how we really feel. There is less need to pretend. He doesn't have to worry about getting every last bit of evidence out of the bathroom sink so I won't know his hair is getting thinner! I don't worry so much about hiding from him the fact that I have to go to more and more trouble to keep looking reasonably attractive!

A big bonus is that we're learning how to play. We like going out to dinner, or off on a lost weekend together. We like it so much that we actually do it instead of just talking about how we ought to do it, like we used to do. We enjoy our children and our friends more. We wish we'd learned to play more freely sooner, for our children's sakes and ours. Our sex life is more fun. We seem more often to experience the "meeting of two solitudes"* and to bridge the gap between our finiteness and the infinite.

Along with learning to satisfy our Child sides more in play and sex, our Parent sides have begun to function more evenly. Howard feels somewhat less the burden of full financial responsibility for the family. That's a shared concern now as I have begun to earn some money, which in turn is satisfying to me. And I feel less emotionally responsible for the family's happiness now that I know he cares as much as I do. We are more able to let each person be the way he or she wants to be.

*Anne Morrow Lindbergh, *Gift from the Sea* (New York: Pantheon, 1955), p. 107.

The strange thing is that along wth our increased closeness and sharing, there is also an enhancement of our separate identities. We are less dependent on each other. For instance, I used to feel deprived, abandoned, and resentful whenever Howard went on one of the trips connected with his work. It's different now. I miss him when he is gone, probably more than I used to. But I do not feel diminished or deserted. Although we are closer than we used to be it is also easier to be separate. That sounds contradictory but it isn't. At the same time that our individuality is enhanced our relationship is strengthened. I feel whole, even when we are not together. It seems to me that a woman (or man) who feels herself a full human being outside any relationship with a man is more apt to feel that way within one.

Since we enjoy each other more in these ways, we also seem to be able to affirm each other more. I remember, in the early years of our marriage, how much Howard wished for more affirmation of his masculinity—his achievements and his humanness—from me. I often couldn't give it to him because, without being aware of it, I felt resentful of the differences in our life satisfactions. Unconsciously, I blamed him for my narrow life—for its lack of stimulation, for my inability to use my talents. And I resented that our marriage, which was my whole life, was only one of many interests for him. I remember how at the same time I wished for more affirmation from him in the form of time and attention. He really couldn't give these, I realize now, because he was so bound up with becoming a success in his work, and because that kind of relationship didn't fit in with his most urgent needs at the time—though part of him was hungry for more of what I needed, too. Since we are becoming more nearly equal partners in a joint venture, we are able to affirm each other more. It's not so much that we care more. We always cared. It is again the feeling of being both less dependent and at the same time more satisfied with our relationship.

It seems to us that the new growth in our marriage has been parallel with beginning to free ourselves from our own narrow expectations of each other and from society's narrow limits to our behavior. Since we no longer believe that women are "supposed" to do one thing and men another, we are less apt to try to fit each other into the old male-female boxes. We are less apt to judge each other for the way we do or do not meet each other's needs. We are more often able to value each other as two human beings stuggling to discover together what life is all about.

Lest it begin to sound as though we have some sort of utopian relationship, I must hasten to add that we still have our ups and downs. There is still conflict—less often than in the past, but sometimes more intense when it arises. There are plenty of times when our individual needs conflict or when both of us get so involved in doing our own thing that our relationship suffers. Then we simply have to work out some kind of compromise. Neither of us can always have everything we want individually and have the kind of relationship we want too. So compromises have to be made on the basis both of what's fair for each of us and what's best for our relationship.

One of the things we have had to do is to divide up the dirty work of daily living—the cooking, the cleaning, the shopping, the yard, the car—all the myriad things that help keep us alive and comfortable. That isn't easy. Before, jobs were well defined, however unfairly. Each knew what was expected. We found that we had literally to rewrite the contract. And we didn't set about doing that until after I'd blown my top a few times and refused to go on being the maintenance and support system for the family any more. When the message finally got through, we sat down to list all the things that have to be done on a regular basis. Then we listed which of those things each of us was actually doing. It turned out to be pretty lopsided; I was, as I suspected, carrying most of the load! So we divided things up more fairly, on the basis of what each of us preferred doing and what neither of us wants to do. It's been a trial and error process. It's taken several rewritings, several new experiments, several explosions of temper from both of us! Each time things work a little more smoothly. At first we tried splitting everything up evenly and taking turns. Now we've decided that it's no use Howard learning to cook or me learning auto mechanics. But he can make a bed and clean up the kitchen and I can remember to get gas and get the oil checked! We still find it best to write out whose job is what, mostly so I'll know what I don't have to feel guilty about, if it isn't done. We've reprogrammed daily responsibilities. He doesn't like that very well and I don't like the way he does his share very well. But, as he says, if he's going to clean up the kitchen he'll do it on his time and by his standards. That's only fair, of course. The trouble is, people who drop by don't leave saying to each other, "Wow, *he's* a sloppy housekeeper." It's hard for me to give up the old ways, or to accept new standards. I have to confess I sometimes remake the bed after he's done it. So this is an area that we are constantly renegotiating. In this case "renegotiate" sometimes means "fight it out."

Sometimes one or the other of us has to give up something we'd like because the needs of the other one seem more important. Sometimes taking turns is the only answer. This is *my* decade for example, and when Howard's needs and mine come into conflict, usually I'm the one who carries the weight. I'm catching up, in the sense of having the opportunity to use myself more fully. Although Howard accepts this (in fact it was his idea), there are times when he is frustrated by it. He's used to having things his way. There is no question that an equalitarian marriage is more difficult because there are fewer automatic guidelines. It's clear to us now that a basic honesty and openness are necessary if growth in this direction is to continue. But to the degree that it has been possible for us to achieve such a relationship, or experience is that it is better.

It used to be so simple to talk about marriage. Boy meets girl; they fall in love; he asks for her hand in marriage; after a suitable interval of playing hard to get, she consents; there is a beautiful wedding; they live happily ever after. Not always, of course. But men and women knew their places. People often made the best of a bad situation. Divorce wasn't an easy option. But though most people are acutely aware that times have changed, as a society we seem still to be expecting traditional or conventional marriages to work for everyone. The evidence is that they aren't working any more for a great many people. Although some couples still stay together "for the sake of the children," or because there isn't enough money for a divorce, or because they're used to each other and afraid of the uncertainty of something new, or because of guilt, or because divorce is forbidden by their religion, the soaring divorce rates suggest that fewer people are willing to put up with unsatisfying relationships. On all sides we hear that marriage is doomed; that the family is breaking down; that people don't care any more about the old values.

But at the same time, marriage rates are also going up! More people are getting married than ever before. Eighty-seven percent of college students list family life among their most important goals.* Apparently it isn't marriage itself that is in question in many cases as much as it is the limited models and cramping definitions of marriage that we still struggle under. People, especially women (but men too), are now looking for greater intimacy in marriage than formerly was the case; they are looking for more fulfilling styles, for richer relationships, for more human satisfactions. This puts a heavier burden on the marriage relationship, one that the traditional style of marriage often cannot bear. Marriage and divorce statistics seem to suggest that as a society we still hope that there is potential fulfillment in marriage; we keep trying! Perhaps we're hoping that somehow in marriage we'll find ourselves not just as robots in roles, but as human beings who need and are needed by each other as human beings.

Marriage is a social as well as a personal institution. It must be affirmed and supported by the institutions and practices of society. But so far our society supports only traditional marriages. That makes it extra difficult for people who believe in marriage but want to try new ways. We need to change both our expectations and limitations.

Change of all kinds is so rapid that it leaves us breathless. Margaret Mead says that all of us born before 1940 are "immigrants in time."** We cannot know what even the next five years will bring in any area of our collective life. We do not know what styles of

*National Institute of Mental Health Study, *Los Angeles Times,* February 11, 1971.
**Margaret Mead, *Culture and Commitment* (New York : Doubleday, 1972), p. 72.

human relationships will emerge as more workable. People are trying many different ways already. Communes, communities, mini-marriages without legal bonds, serial marriage, trial marriage—all seem to be styles that work for some people some of the time. With the population explosion and birth control, women have been freed from lifelong ties to pregnancy and child-rearing. That means we are morally responsible for using our time and intelligence and personalities in other ways that will benefit society. Probably the time has already come when all women need to have at least some interests outside the home for the sake of their own mental health and their husband's physical health as well as the world's social health. This means a revolution in marriage and family styles. For the first time in history, marriage can be approached as an adult relationship for its own sake, rather than as mainly a first step toward building a family. Whatever styles of relationship coming generations may adopt, their needs as human beings for closeness with other human beings will remain. Marriage, or some form of committed relationship of trust and respect and love between a man and a woman, will continue to be needed.

It is my conviction that what is called for now is "liberated marriage," a relationship in which two people who *like* each other, who *love* each other, who are able to have fun together, and to share the transcendent moments of life together, make a conscious commitment to each other and their own growth. They must be able to accept each other's individuality and separateness, to rejoice in the other's achievements as well as in their own, to care for each other, to meet each other's needs as one way of meeting their own, to enjoy sex both deeply and playfully, to enjoy being and becoming human together.

There is as yet little social support for that kind of relationship. Couples who choose to try new ways of relating must expect cultural roadblocks and social disapproval of varying kinds. I shall never forget an audience in England before which Howard and I were engaging in a dialogue. We disagreed about something, as we sometimes do, even in public. A man in the audience suddenly jumped up and shouted at me, "Don't you contradict him!" Equality can be threatening. But all of us who want it can probably achieve a liberated relationship to some degree. To the extent that we can achieve it we will be more human. Such a relationship, in marriage or out of it, is one in which mutuality prevails over hierarchy. True intimacy is impossible where there are rigid lines of command. A liberated relationship must transcend sexual roles and identities. Both man and woman must be strong and weak, leading and loving. The old dominance-submission pattern of marriage in which the man is always the "head of the house" will not work in an equalitarian relationship.

Such a relationship means that the old way of drifting into a marriage without much conscious thought and planning, just assuming things will work out because the roles are well defined, won't work either. A couple will have to create an *intentional marriage,* one in which both partners can love and be loved as individuals wth varied interests and concerns. It will be a relationship simultaneously more spontaneous and more purposeful. It can't "just happen"—especially not between people who are deeply programmed into rigid roles. But it can be cultivated; and it will be freer, more fun, more exhilarating, more stimulating simply because both partners can be *whole.*

That's a great ideal, one which we've been able to reach only partially. But it is an ideal that can be approached in a relationship where the intention is to practice genuine equality and mutual respect, where two people are willing to be themselves and not what society happens to define as maleness or femaleness. Sometimes I speculate about whether such a relationship is harder for young newlyweds or for long marrieds like us. Some things about it are harder for one than the other. Howard and I, for example, struggle with the resistance to changing long-standing feelings, standards, and behavior patterns in our marriage, and that is hard to do. But we do not have the worries about money, small children, and mountains of washing, ironing, cooking, and cleaning that younger couples usually have to contend with. The society does not cooperate with women who want to be fulfilled outside the home, even when husbands do cooperate. Child care, part-time jobs, and schooling are hard to get. Even if a couple decides they want to reverse roles, or share the working and parenting, they often cannot afford to because the husband is the one who is making or can make the most money. Many couples simply have to take turns. Society exacts heavy sacrifices from couples who want to do unapproved things. Although that's changing, the change is much too slow. Only those couples who have enough money, enough education, and certain professional jobs can hope to break out of the traditional pattern completely. And even then it takes some pioneering courage. Someday perhaps the society will allow enough flexibility and variety so that individuals and couples can do what they want to do to express their unique personalities. Meantime, pioneering couples of any age are forced to experiment on their own against the limitations of cultural acceptability.

At the same time there are many possibilities for equalizing relationships if we accept the idea that what we do is not as important as the way we feel about what we do. How a couple manages to work out the maximum satisfactions and growth opportunities of each person is a matter for a particular couple to decide. The wife may stay home while the children are young and the husband work outside the home or vice versa. She may be the breadwinner, or he, or they may share it. Many couples will choose shared responsibility both at home and in the outside world. They may work at the same job or entirely different ones. They may hire child care and housekeeping or share it themselves. They may divide the home and household responsibilities by the hour, the day, the week, month, or year.

We know two young couples with small children who live in one house. They have divided the household responsibilities in two ways. Some are the responsibilities of one couple or the other. Some are responsibilities divided between the two men and the two women. The families live in two different parts of the house but share kitchen, laundry, and cleaning facilities. We know another group of four middle-aged couples whose children are nearly grown who are sharing a huge old house that they remodeled. Each family has its separate quarters. But they cook and eat together, share laundry facilities, yard work, and cars. That is ecologically sound as well as easier and cheaper. Activities are divided according to interest. One couple has charge of the shopping, cooking, and cleaning, because that's what they like to do. All the others are engaged in either volunteer activities or money-making jobs. In both instances, the families involved have the advantages of nuclear family intimacy along with the support and friendship of an extended family and a shared workload. Such couples are still unusual in our society. Most people we know who are trying to develop equalitarian marriages are still doing it within the context of the nuclear family.

There are a few people to whom being human together seems to come naturally. I think of one couple we know who follow traditional lines almost exclusively in what they do. He is a professional man and earns all the money. She is an outstanding homemaker; their home reflects her decorating and artistic and gardening and cooking skills. She is active in many worthwhile volunteer activities. It is quite obvious that she feels "whole." Their children are grown and they can afford to pay for help to do much of the routine work of the house. They do have mutual interests at many points. Though they follow the traditional female and male role patterns, theirs is a relationship of equality because it is one of mutual valuing and respect, one of those rare ones that seems to "just happen."

There are several characteristics of an equalitarian marriage that are important. For most of us, they are qualities that do not come easily but must be worked for. When they can be achieved, they bring with them enough satisfactions in the relationship to more than compensate for the struggle.

I have already spoken of the need for a *conscious contract*. Of course I don't mean the kind of contracting that turns marriage into a business arrangement. But it is a conscious effort on the part of each to be aware of the other's needs and those of the relationship and of how to meet these needs fairly. Some couples find it helpful to write down and divide up daily work responsibility. Others don't need that. But the contract I'm talking about is much more. It is based on a continuing discovery of each other—of the other's needs and resources and the potential of the relationship. It means dealing both with feelings and with specific decisions.

A young couple in my office recently for premarital counseling were talking about their awareness that both wanted to continue in school but somebody needed to work if they were to be married. And what would happen if and when they decided to have children? How would the housekeeping and parenting be divided up? Would it be all her responsibility? Those are the specifics and it is well to deal with them ahead of time. If each goes into the marriage assuming but not being sure that the other is planning to do things a certain way, there is likely to be serious trouble. This is especially crucial as more and more women are questioning traditional role divisions. It's no longer safe to take for granted the old assumption that he will earn money and she will stay home with the children. Not that that pattern is no longer workable; it is for some couples, but the issue had better be discussed ahead of time.

The same couple also needed to deal with their *feelings* about their struggle to work things out fairly for both. He accepted intellectually that she also had a right to continue her education, but he was aware of some resentment and the deep-down feeling that her educational advancement was against the natural order of things! His very recognition of this conflicted feeling and his honesty about it was half the battle. Feelings recognized and dealt with are less apt to sabotage a relationship later. She also felt some resentment that he should feel that way. Fortunately, both were willing to work both on the problem itself and on accepting their own and each other's feelings about the problem. When both partners are willing to negotiate and both are willing to face their anger, frustration, and pain, the chances for working out differences are good.

Of course, on that basis, a contract, even one that has been unconsciously established, can be changed. That's what Howard and I, and many other longer married couples are trying to do. No one contract is good for the lifetime of a marriage unless it can change as needs, interests, and desires change.

That leads to another component of an equalitarian marriage, and that is *flexibility*. It is unlikely that two rigid people, set in their ways, unable to consider alternatives or to take into account the differing needs and ideas and ways of being human of the other person, can make a go of an equalitarian marriage. A couple of generations of raising children in more open relationships may make equalitarian marriage easier to achieve. We are not all flexible, and none of us is flexible all the time. This very inflexibility causes many of today's divorces. Increasingly, as women in particular are deciding that they want more from life and marriage than they are currently getting, they begin to ask for changes or to make them. Some husbands are simply too threatened, too inflexible to tolerate change.

One couple came for counseling because the wife was unhappy. Her husband was saying, "Why can't she be happy? She has everything she wants." He was genuinely bewildered by his wife's discontent. She was too. Both had decided that it was her problem. She must be "sick." It developed simply that she was bored. She hadn't worked outside the home because they didn't need the money and there were children at home. Her husband liked her to be home on weekends and evenings so she had developed few interests of her own. She was stagnating and resenting it. She gradually began to build a life for herself that did not revolve completely around her husband and children. He tried to let her, but he couldn't tolerate it. He couldn't accommodate his granitelike image of what a woman "should" be with her growing need to be a more fulfilled person. By this time she was discovering the satisfactions of some independence, some activities that were her own, some interests she didn't know she had. Reluctantly, they were divorced; it was particularly sad because in many ways they really liked each other. But a partnership isn't possible when one person is inflexible. Many women would simply retreat upon discovering that. This one didn't. More and more women are unwilling to retreat.

On the other hand, not all husbands are so inflexible. Many do begin to change when they realize what the problem is. Then again, some women, having discovered what's wrong with them, become demanding and rigidly impatient. If they are not willing to remain flexible, they risk the marriage. Sometimes, too, inflexibility works the other way. Lately I've known two couples in which the man was dissatisfied with the marital relationship because he felt burdened by a wife who was too dependent on him for all her emotional satisfaction. He experienced this as limiting and constricting and wished that his wife would find some life of her own.

Even in relatively equalitarian marriages, where both partners are willing to let each other be whole, flexibility of personality is a major asset. Rigidity of either role definitions or of feeling simply will not let an equalitarian marriage develop fully. Needs and interests change. New demands on a relationship develop. The unexpected crisis occurs. Both partners must be flexible enough to bend with the storms.

An equalitarian marriage requires *shared leadership* too. I notice that the question which invariably comes up first, particularly from men, is "But who makes the decisions? If there's a disagreement, who gets the final say? That's the man's role!" Many women agree. They always have. Otherwise traditional marriages wouldn't have worked this long. But in an equalitarian marriage such questions are obsolete. In any relationship, even where the two people have a great deal in common, there will be some areas where one is stronger or more competent than the other, or where interests differ. There is no longer a "head of the house." The man as the head and the woman as the heart must fuse. Both must share the leadership and the loving. In an equalitarian relationship, leadership must flow back and forth from one to the other. The emphasis must be not on competition for leadership, but on the smooth meshing of the two people toward their individual and joint goals. If she's more competent and more interested in taking care of the yard, then maybe she takes the leadership there. If he loves to cook and is better at it than she, then perhaps that's his area of leadership. Or vice versa. Not that he won't mow the lawn once in a while or she won't cook dinner, or that they won't hire the whole business done if they prefer and can afford it. But each takes responsibility in his or her bailiwick.

The same can be true in parenting. I know one couple in which the father is far more comfortable with small children and the more in tune with adolescents. Since their marriage is a fairly equal relationship, without much conscious planning he automatically took over in areas of leadership when the children were younger; now that they are older, the mother has slipped comfortably into the leadership role. Not that either abdicated from a relationship with the children at any age. But when issues of decision and discipline arose when the children were little, the father felt comfortable making the decisions. That role gradually passed to the mother as they got older. And it was a great experience for the children. Often of course, there were joint decisions when both felt adequate in a particular situation.

Shared leadership is not necessarily 50–50 leadership—probably not even desirably so. Although the couple may choose to divide up specific tasks systematically, each is both free and responsible for pitching in when the other is under pressure; in a relationship where people are mature enough to focus on what's best for the relationship as well as for the individuals the leadership is flexible. Not that they never fight. A lively relationship has plenty of conflict, maybe even thrives on it. But in areas where there is conflict, and leadership does not flow easily negotiation is possible while dealing with the conflict. Negotiation is only possible, however, when both are *committed strongly to the relationship and its growth as well as to their own individual needs and personal growth.* Sometimes negotiation means taking turns. Or sometimes the needs of one are obviously more crucial. Sometimes the needs of the relationship come first, like last weekend when both Howard and I gave up what we each wanted to do and went off together.

I can hear a chorus of "Buts " just now. "But, what happens if both are involved in a career and one gets a better job and wants to move and the other doesn't?" Well, that happens, of course and some marriages break up over it. Traditionally it has been the husband who prevailed in any kind of conflict. Wives are expected to place love and husband and deference to his success above any personal desire for self-fulflllment. Most women have simply gone along, even when they were miserable about it, whether they were leaving careers, or homes and friends. Often husbands have felt guilty about uprooting the family and have chosen not to go, all the while resenting it. In any case, unless both want it there is bound to be friction. The key in an equalitarian marriage is that the needs of both have equal consideration, along with the commitment of both to the relationship. That becomes more possible as men begin to feel as much satisfaction in relationships as they do in job success.

Howard and I have faced the situation many times. Sometimes we both wanted to go. Sometimes I didn't. Sometimes we went anyway. Then he felt guilty. Sometimes I said, particularly in recent years, "No, I'm not going!" And we didn't go. Then I felt guilty. What we now try to do is to say, "What's fair? What's best for both of us and our marriage? What sacrifices will either of us have to make?" It's always a painful decision, but we end up liking each other better and with neither of us feeling overwhelmed by resentment and guilt. Shared leadership is a vital part of all aspects of an equalitarian marriage.

A fourth need in equal marriages is for each partner to be able to maintain and develop his and her *separate identity*. Each must be able to respect and take pleasure in the other's fulfillment. The equalitarian marriage cannot assume that one or the other partner's self-fulfillment is more important. In the past many women were fulfilled in their roles as wife and mother and some will continue to be. But nearly all women will increasingly need some interests that are their own. As productive work in the sense of making more things to expand the economy becomes less and less necessary or even possible, there will be more and more need for the creative use of leisure. Many women will be among the artists and writers and musicians of the future. Whatever women who choose homemaking decide to do with the time they have outside of child-rearing must be valued in the relationship. What seems likely is that women and men will increasingly share the work interests and creative interests both within the home and out of it. Within a relationship where two people must affirm their individuality and their humanity, the needs and desires of both must be respected. And that takes some negotiation and often some compromise.

Commitment is a fifth component of equalitarian marriage. It's one that runs like a thread through all the others and through the relationship. Without it there can be no truly equal relationship. In the past, commitment has often meant possession. Although that has most often meant that the man possesses the woman (the word "obey" has only recently come out of some religious wedding ceremonies, and it is still in some) in feeling and practice, it has often worked both ways. The traditional night before the wedding stag party, where the male enjoys his freedom for the last time, illustrates this. Many jokes about men getting trapped into marriage, henpecked husbands, demanding wives, marriage as a life sentence for a man, are other illustrations. The other side is reflected in the woman's loss of her name, being given away by her father (woman as property, again), the assumption that a woman must wear a wedding ring but the man need not unless he chooses, the use of titles to designate marital status for women but not for men. So both sexes have often traditionally both viewed and experienced marriage as limiting rather than expanding, as imprisoning rather than freeing, as "possessed by" rather than "committed to."

Equalitarian marriage has the potential of a far richer and more satisfying form of committed relationship. It emphasizes the commitment to the relationship and to the growth of each person, rather than a giving up of one person's freedom. It is the sort of commitment that leaves each one free to become as fully human as he or she can, to engage in activities, both work and play, that interest him or her, and to be free to exercise whatever attitudes and tastes come naturally without any particular definition as to whether they're masculine or feminine or not. The commitment, in other words, is both to the development of the two individuals in the relationship and to the relationship itself. It must be a *constantly renewed commitment.* Most couples in such a relationship from time to time ask the questions, "How are we doing? Are we meeting each other's needs? Are we feeling good about our separate identities and good about our relationship?"

Commitment in an equal marriage also means that each person is as committed to the other's humanity and its development as to his or her own. It's the kind of commitment that makes negotiation easier during conflicts because each feels strongly about the satisfactions of the relationship. That means that the joys in the relationship must be great enough to make possible a certain amount of sacrifice on the part of each person. There will always be times when individual fulfillment and development of the relationship seem incompatible. Some marriages will end when individual needs seem more important than and collide with relationship ones. But the satisfactions of an equalitarian relationship are so great once they are experienced that commitment is apt to be natural and honest. Staying together because you're stuck with each other and staying together because you choose to are different matters.

Recently Howard and I participated in a wedding ceremony in which the young couple said to each other as they exchanged rings, "Now I will be thy forever friend." Equalitarian marriage makes it possible for two people to be "forever friends" as well as lovers. But it requires a kind of openness and honesty and trust that are impossible in a dominance-submission relationship. It's a kind of openness that allows each person to drop his or her defenses, to give up pretending that he or she is not vulnerable. It's the kind of openness and honesty that lets me know that I can share my doubts about my femininity and my fears of growing old with my husband without losing his love. In the same way, he can admit to himself and to me that often he isn't so sure of himself either. Such openness means that we can give up many of the rituals that have defined us as female and male instead of as persons, and have therefore kept us apart. We can allow ourselves to be more fully known by the other in a variety of ways—physically, and psychologically, with all our weaknesses and shortcomings. It's the kind of openness that makes the whole range of human emotions available to both of us—fear, anger, pain, love, joy, happiness—sometimes we make each other miserable, sometimes joyful. Mostly we make each other aware of being alive!

A few years ago, Howard and I wrote a book* in which we

---

*Clinebell and Clinebell, *The Intimate Marriage* (New York: Harper & Row, 1970).

described various methods of deepening relationships. It's full of ideas about becoming human together, though it doesn't use those words. We still affirm what it says about communication, mutual need satisfaction, and the enriching of marriage. It recognizes the importance of changing roles and equality in marriage, but it was written before we had fully appreciated in a personal way the tremendous importance of these issues to a deep intimacy. Equality now seems to us to be the very foundation on which an intimate marriage or any other kind of female-male relationship must be built. A liberated marriage is an equal one, in which husband and wife are willing to meet in the middle.

Some people feel that with the steadily lengthening life expectancy for women and men, it's unrealistic to expect that very many couples can stand each other, must less enjoy each other, for a lifetime. Certainly it's already true that a lot of people don't. Abraham Maslow, on the other hand, has found that in self-actualizing people, love and sex satisfactions improve with the age of the relationship.* Since it is more possible to become self-actualized in a relationship of equality, it seems likely that as more whole human beings, female and male, develop, more relationships of depth over long periods of time will become possible.

Howard and I have found that as we have become freer people individually, less hung up on what women are supposed to do and what men are supposed to do, we just plain like each other better. The awakening in me to which he has responded positively has awakened our relationship as well. A friend of ours who did not get to live out her full life span said before she died, "I've got so much more living to do!" That is exactly the feeling we have. A marriage of equality, of interdependence—an *intentional* relationship—is a growing one, a life-affirming one, one in which there can be so much more living, both individually and together. Marriage seems to us to be the place where it is most possible to meet in the middle.

*Abraham Maslow, *Motivation and Personality,* (Harper & Row, 1954), p. 239.

Five / Liberated Sex

Many couples have some sort of hilarious or hair-raising or hurting (or some combination of those) honeymoon story to tell. Ours is a post–honeymoon story. Our first home as newlyweds was a small apartment high in the belfry of a big midwestern church where Howard was on the staff as associate minister. It was July and very hot for sleeping way up in an almost unventilated tower. So we moved an old mattress two floors down to the Junior Department and there we slept when the nights were bad. One particularly hot night we had gone to bed on our mattress without benefit of pajamas or nightie or sheet in order to make the most of whatever slight breeze should manage to blow through. We fell asleep in spite of the heat. Suddenly in the darkness a floodlight shone upon us. We scrambled for the sheet, guiltily aware that two burly policemen were staring down at us! Of course they began at once to ask questions. And of course, they didn't believe us until Howard took them to our belfry and showed them our marriage license. I suppose it did look a little odd to see two unclothed kids asleep in the Junior Department at 3 A.M.! I was scared; Howard was angry! It wasn't funny till the next day. As it turned out, the policemen had seen our little 1927 rumble-seated Dodge parked in the street in front of the church. Howard had forgotten to put it away (the car was his responsibility). And those two great big policemen had squeezed through a tiny open window to search the church, expecting to catch a vandal or two. The story has supplied us and our friends with many a good laugh over the years. But it has its sad side too. Because what I remember best is the guilt I felt even though I had a marriage license to show. To be caught in bed with a man! And in a church, besides!

I remember standing at the foot of the stairs while Howard took the policemen up to see our house and license, and I couldn't look them in the eye as they came down, apologizing. I've often wondered what they said to each other about it all afterward. They did have the grace to be embarrassed after they were convinced that we were not behaving sinfully, but that didn't stop them from giving us a ticket for parking illegally in the street at night! I felt both guilty and punished!

"Nice girls don't!" Certainly never before marriage and afterward only if they don't enjoy it too much. Guilt and sex have been synonymous for many women for generations. The double standard has given men more freedom; premarital and extramarital sex for men have long been outwardly frowned on but slyly winked at. Thus, in spite of their greater freedom, many men have grown up also feeling guilty about sex.

So in many ways the fresh wind generated by a new openness toward sexual matters and the remarkable scientific discoveries about sexuality is both long overdue and welcome. New understandings about women's sexual capacity, easier and safer birth control methods, have helped to free both sexes from crippling myths about women and sex on the one hand and longstanding worries about pregnancy on the other. Those two major changes throw a whole new light on male-female sexual relationships. Add to those factors the developing equality between the sexes and the ingredients for liberated sex and liberating sex are present.

The kind of female-male equality that this book is all about is the basis for liberated sex. By liberated sex I don't mean sexual license or free love. Liberated sex is "a free, spontaneous, primitive sexual response between men and women who look on each other as individuals rather than as walking stereotypes."* Primitive simply means that we are free to be ourselves without being boxed in by rigid rules of masculinity and femininity, and free to enjoy the lusty,

*Myron Brenton, *The American Male* (New York: Coward–McCann, 1966), p. 191.

sensuous side of ourselves and each other. Sexual liberation is simply one important aspect of total human liberation. It means that as women and men we treat each other as human beings rather than only as sex objects or as instruments for selfish gratification. Sexual liberation will not be achieved by itself in isolation from the liberating human relationship that gives sex its meaning.

The physiological findings of Masters and Johnson have freed many women and men to enjoy sex more completely. They have made us aware once and for all that women as well as men can have richly satisfying sex lives. Many men and women are finding that in a relationship of equality, liberated sex is possible—that they can luxuriate in what feels natural and good and satisfying for the two people involved. Men and women can express their sexual needs to each other without fear of being either too aggressive or too demanding. They can engage in the kinds of activities that meet their own desires and needs rather than having these activities determined by some outside cultural criteria for what is "proper" or what is "masculine" or "feminine." Liberated sex means an end to the double standard about who can enjoy sex and who can't, and how much, or who can initiate sex and who can't. It means an end also to the dehumanizing effect of the double standard, which detaches sex from a relationship of respect and caring. It means an end to "nice girls don't" and "real men must." It means an end to the demand quality of performance for both men and women. It means, in short, relax and enjoy—each other and sex.

There is no doubt that the new openness and the new discoveries about sex, along with the new equality between women and men, are providing a solid basis for increased sexual pleasure and spontaneity. Unfortunately there are also some pitfalls in the new approach. For many women and men the new and exciting knowledge about woman's sexual capacity has increased rather than decreased the demand quality in sexual relationships. It is not the knowledge itself, but the fact that we have not changed our feelings and attitudes in ways that free us to enjoy the new knowledge. Science has freed us from old stereotypes, but we were raised by them and to a great extent continue to raise our children by them. So although we now know that women have capacity for sexual pleasure at least as great as men's, along with the added possibility of multiple orgasms, we also continue to teach our young females that "nice girls don't" until after marriage. Then, according to the new knowledge, they must be wildly abandoned in bed and are not fully successful unless they have multiple orgasms.

The old way, though destructive, was at least consistent. Then, as now, we taught girls to be as sexy as possible but not to indulge in or enjoy sex until after marriage. Victorian mores taught girls that after marriage they were to tolerate sex, to "do their duty" by their husbands, but not to enjoy it too much. It wasn't ladylike. Later generations, mine for example, were taught that sex *should* be pleasurable for women after marriage but that women were basically not as interested in sex as men. Society has traditionally put girls and women in an intolerable double bind by saying to them, "Attract men, but be a nice girl," by "nice" meaning don't enjoy sex too much. Though that method has deprived generations of women of full sexual enjoyment, at least there was less pressure on them. Nowadays as a society we are asking girls to spend the first twenty years of their lives being sexually attractive, but not sexually active, and then after marriage to start suddenly enjoying sex. It's too much to ask. It's no wonder that women seek frantically for ways to be sexually successful. We now demand performance of women as well as of men.

Though in some areas the cultural sanctions against premarital sex are changing even for girls, and although many girls are rejecting the double bind, often they are not truly liberated. There is good evidence* that many girls who do defy convention retain the guilt and ambivalence about sex and about their actions that women have traditionally felt. For all too many such "liberated" young women and their partners, sex remains a diminishing and dehumanizing experience. New discoveries and freedom from pregnancy have given them license but not inner freedom.

Girls grow up feeling ambivalent and confused about sex and

*Judith Bardwick, *The Psychology of Women* (New York: Harper & Row, 1971).

about their bodies. That too, makes it hard for them as women to switch from repressing sexual feelings to expressing them. The vagina is associated with bleeding, often with menstrual pain, and with fears of the possible pain of childbirth for most girls. Unlike boys, who discover the sexual pleasure of the penis at an early age, girls frequently do not become aware of the clitoris and its potential until after puberty, and often not then. The physical and anatomical realities in the context of a society that says girls are not supposed to experience sexual pleasure until they are grown and married effectively programs masses of women for frigidity. So it is not really surprising that the new discoveries about women's capacity for sexual pleasure are all too often a threat instead of a joy, a load instead of liberation. The good news is bad news for many. It only makes them aware of what they're missing.

There is some evidence that the patriarchal system with its subjugation of women came about over a period of five thousand years between 12000 and 8000 B.C.* Some anthropological evidence indicates that in the dawn of history, women enjoyed complete sexual freedom and were sexually insatiable. But with the beginnings of civilization and the development of family life, society found it necessary to limit women; they could no longer be promiscuous, satisfying their sexual needs at any time or place if the laws of paternity and a stable community were to develop. In the process of bringing the sexual drive of women under control, all kinds of other controls upon women developed as well. So civilization has spent maybe ten thousand years repressing and keeping repressed women's natural sexual capacity. No wonder we have such a hard time becoming "multiply orgasmic" again! Not only the first twenty years of a woman's life are spent repressing her sexuality, but she is also the product of thousands of years of such repression.

And what about men? They also are experiencing the threat of change. The old way had its problems. The performance-demand

---

*Mary Jane Sherfey, *The Evolution and Nature of Female Sexuality* (New York: Random House, 1972), p. 138.

quality for men and boys and the depersonalizing of women as sex objects has been deeply destructive, both to men and to male-female relationships. But for men as well as for women, at least the old way was clear. Men were supposed to be on top, in all ways. Both sexes knew what to expect and how to behave. But in the same way that we have created a new sexual burden for women, we have added to the male burden. We are now saying to boys and men, not only is your own sexual performance a requirement, but you are responsible for seeing that your mate has many orgasms, too.

The change in women's sexual behavior is particularly threatening for many men, and has put them in a new bind. They have in the past been expected to be sexually virile at all times, and at the same time to be successful on the job. That wasn't so bad as long as the patriarchal stand was unquestioned, and men made the decisions about how much sex, what kind, and when. But now that the double standard is breaking down, and women are demanding full sexual equality and enjoyment, it's men who have to adjust and adapt. Although the dominant position of males precluded depth intimacy, at least men felt more secure. They could initiate sex when they felt like it without fear of being unready. Now that women can also initiate and feel "a right" to sexual satisfaction, many men are under even more pressure. They are put to the test every time intercourse takes place in a way that females are not. What a terrible burden that can be for a man! A woman can fake sexual success. A man cannot.

Knowledge that the female sex drive is as strong as or even stronger than the male's, and awareness that the society is increasingly affirming women's right to be as sexually emancipated as men, also adds new pressures for some men. Recent experience in marriage counseling suggests that because of these pressures sexual apathy and impotence are on the increase among men. Or at least men now are more willing to talk about it. Women who take the sexual initiative, however subtly, are a threat to many men because they increase the performance demand. Some men are frightened and retreat into preoccupation with their work, where they know they can be successful, or at least on top of the pecking order; or they become domineering, insisting that their partners continue to play the old submissive role; or they turn to other women who will conform by being submissive or nurturing or mothering. Some men just live on in quiet desperation, feeling like failures.

The essentially freeing development of the birth control pill has its negative side as well, unfortunately. For one thing, all too often men assume that a "liberated" woman is one who is now free to have sex any time and with any man because she does not have to be afraid of getting pregnant. I am continually surprised by the number of young women who feel that now they are expected to be sexually available and are afraid of losing a relationship with a man if they refuse. It is as though they no longer have an excuse. At the same time they feel they will also lose the man's respect, and therefore the man, if they cooperate. Another double bind.

Ambivalence about both the pleasure of sex and about the morality of it sometimes become more complicated when women are "freed" by the Pill. Some women get enough pleasure from sex and have high enough self-esteem that they are not so apt to feel used. But for most women, romance and spontaneity are important and taking the Pill as a conscious act when sex isn't even being considered takes away some of that spontaneous response. Many women, married and unmarried, seem to feel that making themselves available at all times by taking the Pill is somehow immoral, that they are prostituting themselves. These are often unconscious feelings and will change as we begin to raise girls differently. Meanwhile, if they are present, they get in the way of full sexual enjoyment for women and indicate that the Pill is not as freeing as it could be.

The Pill is by far the surest method of contraception yet devised. But the psychological and physical factors, some known and some unknown, raise serious questions. Side effects such as weight gain, nausea, and swelling breasts are unpleasant, if not unhealthy. There is increasing evidence, too, that sexual desire in some women is inhibited by the Pill. Whether that is widespread, whether it is caused by physical factors or psychological ones such as those mentioned above, it's an important issue. The major unknown factor is the question of what happens with long-term use of the Pill. So far, only about fifteen years have gone by since American women began to use it regularly. What happens to female life expectancy, for example, if a woman uses the Pill for all of her fertile years? We just don't know that yet.

Caution is required with any form of birth control that causes major changes in the natural physiological processes, as the Pill does. My doctor said to me, "When you see the changes it makes in a woman's body, the side effects, the way it delays menopause and slows down some of the physical symptoms of aging, you know it isn't just an aspirin tablet."

But the issue of contraception or birth control is a vital one in any discussion of sexual liberation. One of the major reasons we can talk about sexual equality at all is that pregnancy has become optional. Women need not (in fact must not) spend their lives being barefoot in summer and pregnant in winter! A number of touchy questions are raised by this remarkable fact.

A basic right for all human beings, male or female, is control of our own bodies. No man should be required to have a vasectomy if he doesn't want it. No woman should face a sterilizing procedure if she doesn't want it. No woman should be forced to bear a child she doesn't want or not to bear a child she does want. It is to be hoped that we will be able to bring the world's population under control before mandatory birth control methods become necessary. If we cannot, we face the possibility of government control of sterilization and abortion for the regulation of birth.

Sex cannot be "liberated" for either men or women unless it is possible to prevent pregnancy or to terminate it when it happens. Traditionally it has been the responsibility of women to prevent unwanted pregnancy or to bear the consequences. This is true in wedlock and out of it. Young girls are responsible for seeing that young men don't "go too far." In spite of changing sexual mores that is still true. Most married women are responsible for the couple's birth control.

We are only beginning to hear the call for more research on male contraception—short of vasectomy. Probably 99 percent of research on contraception is directed toward the female. Since women are the ones who get pregnant, no doubt that has seemed logical in the past. It has only lately occurred to anyone that maybe there is an effective method of birth control through the male body. (The condom is neither fully effective nor satisfying.) There is a healthy trend toward more vasectomies among married men with children. But a vasectomy is nearly always final, so that it can never be a method of birth control for all men.

Perhaps it is true, as some say, that male scientists and doctors are less willing to tamper with the male body than they are with the female. There has been enough study to make it obvious that a male pill is possible; it has been tried *on convicts,* but it interfered with their toleration for alcohol! A device to control the flow of sperm has been developed, (but not perfected) for implanting in the male body. Some of these signs are hopeful. Someday we will find a method of contraception for one or both sexes that is both safe to use and without negative side effects. But that probably won't happen until men feel equally responsible for choosing or preventing pregnancy. Fully liberated sex is possible only when the prevention and the planning of pregnancy are fully acceptable and felt as the joint responsibility of both women and men.

As a society we are preoccupied with sex. We have swung from the good old Victorian days when even pianos couldn't have legs to twenty-four-hour-a-day sex in the living room. Television, books, magazines, radio, newspapers, movies, continuously hawk their sexual wares to an insatiable public. Women are enjoined to wash their hair daily, to smell heavenly, to use the right detergent and the right coffee and the right furniture polish so that a man will say, "I think I'll keep her!" Men are urged to smoke the right cigarette while riding a horse in the country or while driving the right car, and lately, to smell sweet at the same time in order to appear masculine and desirable to women. We are bombarded with admonitions to stay or to become sexually irresistible. The prevailing voices seem to be saying to women "Are you a good lay?" and to men, "Can you lay 'em good?'' We have made sex objects of *both* men and women.*

In more serious ways we are also preoccupied with sex. Dozens of books are published yearly on the pros and cons and the mechanics of sex, whether there should be sex education in the schools, or in the homes, or whether there should be any at all. We worry about obscenity and pornography and the *Playboy* philosophy. We argue about whether anything goes between consenting adults or whether the law should decide what we can and cannot do and read and see. We have taken the whole issue to the Supreme Court several times, in various forms; they seem as confused about it all as the rest of us. Clearly we have overloaded the sexual circuits.

The high anxiety in both men and women surrounding sexual performance is aggravated by this overloading. The other day, Howard recalled a tired, tail-dragging couple he saw recently at the beach. They were obviously not enjoying each other—at the moment at least. The man was clutching a best seller on the mechanics of sex, perhaps part of a vain hope that he could recapture the long-lost spark. That started us talking about the early days of our marriage. Those were the times of the "holy, holy, holy" marriage manuals. After much reading of such manuals, we used to wonder why the bells weren't ringing and the skies falling. Those were the days of awareness that women were "supposed" to have an orgasm, preferably a vaginal one, preferably without manual stimulation, and preferably simultaneously with their mates. And it was felt to be the young husband's responsibility to discover the kind of foreplay that would arouse the latent sexuality of a guilty young wife who deep down believed that sex was wrong, even in marriage. How hard we tried, and how disappointed we were when we couldn't make the ecstatic experiences of simultaneous, fifty-fifty orgasm happen. And how long it took us to discover, by trial and error, that what I most needed was to *learn* what an orgasm was for me, and how to achieve it, and what we both most needed was to treat each other as two human beings. Instead, for too long we were dominated by

*Brenton, *op. cit.,* p. 182.

the "tyranny of the female orgasm"—what we thought *ought* to happen.

I am not suggesting that it isn't ever helpful to read. It is. The more accurate knowledge and inspired encouragement we can get as human beings, the better. But our cultural preoccupation with sex reflects our collective disappointment with our failure to attain true sexual intimacy. Good sex, like good food, is something that healthy people anticipate with pleasure, enjoy fully when it happens, but does not become an obsession. Our current cultural obsesssion demands inhuman attention to sex and inhuman performance from both women and men. Sex would be more satisfying and more fun if we could relax and enjoy it with fewer demands and fewer rules and regulations about what sexual fulfillment is.

> I have a fondness for cookbooks that do not make one feel as though the soufflé will fall if the sugar is a quarter of a teaspoon off. I rather like the ones that say: add a little oregano, parsley will do it, but on the other hand, the whole thing will taste perfectly okay if you just stick in some salt and pepper.
>
> Maybe there could be a book like that. Maybe both sexes could get a little rest for a while. And we might get a little of the real pleasure that comes from relaxing, and accepting ourselves in all our delightful diversity.*

That's what liberated sex is—relaxing and accepting ourselves and each other in all our "delightful diversity." With the rise of sexual equality, sexual liberation is also possible. Since we no longer need to view males as dominant and all-powerful and females as weak and submissive, we can enjoy our sexual difference more fully. We can give up the Parent-Child games that make sex less mutually satisfying. The dominance-submission or Parent-Child ways of relating that this book has been talking about get in the way of good sex. The anger women feel at being one down complicates sexual relationships with men. It's pretty hard to enjoy sex with someone who is exploiting you, however unconsciously. Women have often withheld sex as

*Carol Rinzler, *Ms.*, June 1972, p. 118.

one of the few powers they have over men. When power is equal, that method is unnecessary. Very often frigidity can be defined as "frozen anger." Howard and I have found that giving up the Parent-Child relationship and interacting as two equal human beings has freed our sex life tremendously. It's much more interesting, varied, and exciting for both of us chiefly because anger and exploitation don't get in the way. We can enjoy sex more because we can enjoy each other more.

One big gain for both men and women in liberated sex is that we can let go of the body image problem that has put undue pressure on all of us. Of course it hits women harder because physical requirements for the sexually attractive woman are more rigid than for a man. Some women diet frantically and spend fortunes on the cosmetics that they hope will turn them into the sort of sex object that will have power over men's sexual responses. Other women go to the other extreme, rejecting the sex objectification of their bodies, their femininity (perhaps the phony femininity defined by society), by eating compulsively and becoming fat slobs. Somewhere between are most of us who worry about how we look, teeter-totter between dieting and not dieting, spend more time and money than we need to or can afford on cosmetics, trying to remain sexually attractive and still be human. But the only sound basis for diet and exercise and body care is the affirmation and appreciation of oneself as a human being, which makes us want to be healthy, live a long time and be reasonably good to look at. Good sex isn't dependent on having a body like Aphrodite or Apollo. It is dependent on feeling good about oneself. And if we feel good about ourselves we take care of our bodies.

As women and men we can be free as we have never been before from the "tyranny of the orgasm." Isn't it a relief to know that there isn't any right way to enjoy sex, that "the liberated orgasm is any orgasm *you* like under any circumstances *you* find comfortable."* That doesn't mean license or an end to sexual responsibility. It means

*Barbara Seaman, *Free and Female* (New York: Coward, McCann, 1972).

that the frequency of orgasm, the number of orgasms, how they are achieved (manually or during intercourse), and simultaneous orgasm are not issues. It means that sex can be enjoyable *without* orgasm. Relax and enjoy! What's right for you is right! Give up the oughts and shoulds about what is satisfying sex.

Liberated sex means people don't *have* to always succeed in having an orgasm. They can be tired or depressed sometimes without either being a failure or feeling rejected by the other. It means that although the sexual relationship may change over time, the inroads of age will be much less threatening. Sex becomes important *in a relationship* and that means the *persons* are important as well as the sex itself. There are already many women and men who enjoy a liberated sexual relationship within the context of a humanizing relationship. More of us can develop such relationships as we begin to give up old dominant-submissive ways and Parent-Child games and use the marvelous new insights and discoveries about female and male sexuality and the new freedom to be whole. It seems so sad, so ironic, that in the one area where our difference is most obvious and potentially ecstatic, many of us have succeeded in increasing the distance between us as sexes, and increasing our fear of each other.

Yet we have the capacity to pleasure each other so deeply. How tragic that the marvelous sexual capacity of the male is diminished because he is so often on the defensive. How tragic that the marvelous sexual capacity of the female is so often unawakened because it has been so long repressed. How can we relate to each other so that we both give and receive the sexual joy that is our heritage as human beings?

The chief way is to change our traditional view of each other as "male" and "female" cutouts and to see each other as equal human beings. Another is to change the way we raise our children sexually. It may take us a generation or two to undo generations of teaching both girls and boys that women are not as interested in sex as men and that men are always "at the ready." We must find ways of teaching girls how to awaken their sexuality so that they can easily achieve sexual satisfaction when they want it. Many women don't know how to have an orgasm or what gives them pleasure sexually. And they are afraid to find out so that they can teach it to their sexual partners. (Masters and Johnson teach women how to masturbate.) Way down deep, sexual experimentation and pleasure are still "wrong" for many women. We women must change that for ourselves and for our daughters. We must find ways to help girls with the ambivalence they feel about their bodies, and that means demystifying menstruation and childbirth and teaching childbirth without fear. (It also means educating more female gynecologists and obstetricians.)

We must find ways to help boys understand those same biological processes so that they do not grow up fearing women because of the magic powers associated with menstruation and childbirth. In every area, including sex, we must help boys and girls understand and accept each other as biologically different but equally valuable.

It's pretty hard to raise liberated children until we become liberated ourselves. Many people are finding ways to begin. But even children who grow up in homes where sex is a natural and joyful part of life are daily bombarded by our culture's unhealthy attitudes. The ongoing controversy over the place and the value of sex education reflects our continuing confusion between Victorian repression and modern license. Somehow we will have to begin to teach children both the newly discovered facts about sexuality and new attitudes within which to make the facts a healthy part of life.

We are liberated sexually only when as men and women we can share fully both the joys and the responsibilities of sex. Liberated sex, and the capacity to be human together, will develop as we learn to affirm ourselves as uniquely male or female and to affirm each other in the same way. We need a new and more humanizing sexual ethic. The vestiges of Victorian shame and the rigid, repressive attitudes of the past must go. But the new ethic, under the banner of sexual freedom, can cause untold pain and justify much human exploitation. Sex is a tremendously important source of satisfaction. But it is not the only one nor even the most trustworthy. We need a new morality, one that affirms sex in any relationship according to whether it enhances human values and supports and increases both self-esteem and esteem for the other. That is true sexual liberation. Sex is the one area where our uniqueness as females and males is clear. Liberated sex can let us forget our differences and enjoy our differentness!

Six / Liberated Childhood

Sometimes when my resistance to sitting down at the typewriter is overwhelming, I sit down at the piano instead. Just now I did that. To my surprise, what came out of my fingers was the tune, "How dear to my heart are the scenes of my childhood, when fond recollection presents them to view. . . ." My memories are not of an "old oaken bucket" or the "green tangled wildwood," but of a walnut tree to climb, and a playhouse, and the blackberries my father grew and picked for my mother to make jelly from. Many memories are "dear to my heart." Others are painful. I often wonder how it will be with my children when they reach middle age and look backward. Will they remember the joy as well as the pain? Such thoughts reflect my uncertainty about my success as a mother, I guess.

Most of us look back on childhood with a mixture of pleasure and pain, of nostalgia and regret. In an intricate way we are all the products of our genetic heritage, of our childhood experience, and of what we ourselves have made of our lives by hundreds of daily choices. We can't blame our parents, our culture, or our heredity—or give them all the credit either—for whatever is good or bad in our lives.

Yet there is great power for good and ill in the particular cultural setting into which we are born. Our parents are also deeply imprinted by that setting, and we experience the culture screened through them. So it is difficult to tell in which ways our strengths and weaknesses are the result of our unique individual response and experience and which the result of the cultural air that they and we breathe. Parents *are* a powerful influence in helping children to grow up whole. If children see their parents valuing each other equally, if they see them engaging in activities according to their interests, rather than according to arbitrary sex roles, they are likely to grow up to do the same. But we cannot blame parents alone, either our own parents or ourselves as parents. All adults are part of the culture in which they became adults. And all the institutionalized practices of our society help to mold and shape us to fit established stereotypes.

The five-year-old daughter of a friend of mine came home from school one day and announced that she wanted to be a nurse. Her mother said, "Why not a doctor?" Little Tina replied, "Oh, no! Doctors are boys!" Her liberated mother was crushed! All that good home influence wiped out by outside forces! Not really, of course. The open atmosphere at home and Tina's own intelligence will probably prevail in later decisions. But it would help if society supported her right to be and become whatever she can.

Children, like adults, must have the freedom to become fully human without the imprisoning cultural boxes of maleness or femaleness, blackness or whiteness, economic deprivation or any other arbitrary societal limitation. A liberated child is one who is developing an *independent sense of self and an ability to form intimate relationships.* He or she is a child who is glad to be the male or female that he or she is. The child finds its sex not a limiting but an affirming basis for its individual personality. The child is beginning to discover what its own inner self is like, and to affirm it, whatever it is. It is beginning to discover what its innate differences from other people are, whatever the sex. It is beginning to discover what it means to be male or female and to affirm both.* A little girl is beginning to understand what it means to be a female biologically and to look forward to her biological role, however she may someday choose to fulfill it. She is also discovering that her biological role doesn't mean there are only some things she can do and many others she can't simple because she is a girl. All of the same is true for a boy.

*Did you notice I changed from "he or she" to "it"? Not so good, because "it" is for objects. But at least "it" includes both sexes—the subtle power of language.

An independent sense of self means discovering oneself as a human being first, and then as a female or a male. A girl is finding that her sense of wholeness and identity does not depend solely on cultivating a "need to be needed." A boy is discovering that success and achievement are not the only satisfactions in life. Both are learning that the need to give and receive love and the need to feel "successful" or worthwhile are human traits that can be cultivated in a variety of ways not restricted to one sex alone.

Over the years as a mother, a music teacher, a den mother, a Sunday school teacher, and, more recently, as a child therapist, I've known and worked with and loved many children. And I have many vivid memories of my own childhood. These experiences convince me that our society does not provide a fertile soil for cultivating liberated children who will become liberated adults. On the contrary, our society seems to produce relatively few people who are "whole" in the sense that they are able to use their full potential both intellectually and interpersonally.

Two incidents from the play therapy room come to my mind. Ten-year-old Alice, a "dainty, gentle, soft" girl came for help because her parents and teachers thought she was too withdrawn and couldn't make friends. In the playroom she played with the dolls and the dishes, and sometimes the paints. One day she wandered around the room unable to make up her mind what she wanted to do. Presently she was standing above the cars and trucks that covered the floor in one corner of the room. She looked down at them silently for a few moments; then with her toe she tentatively began to shove the big tank truck along the floor. With a sigh she remarked, "I wish it was okay for girls to play with trucks."

Then there was seven-year-old Joey. Joey was an "active, aggressive, noisy" boy who had come for help because he was often violent with other children and disrespectful to adults. One day upon entering the playroom he went at once to the house corner, which he had never touched before, and leaned against the wall gazing at the dolls and dishes and dress-up clothes. He asked me if it was really true that nobody would know about what he did in this room, (something children are always assured of but don't always believe).

Then he turned to the darts for a while but soon came back to look at the doll things in what seemed to me to be a wistful way. So I took a chance and said, "I get the feeling you'd really like to play in the house corner today." To which he replied, "Are you sure you won't tell anyone?"

It's not easy to be a child of either sex. Children are hurt very early by many things. Some are crippled for life by poverty, ignorance, fear, and emotional or physical pain. Our rigid expectations of what's okay for boys and what's okay for girls is crippling too. It shows in homes, classrooms, and on playgrounds as well as in play therapy rooms. An image that comes to me just now is of the tiny bound feet of a Chinese baby. Though that practice has disappeared, most cultures still bind the spirits of children in many ways. Girls are bound tighter than boys, particularly when it comes to passivity and aggressiveness and life choices.

Very early, girls know that they are to be compliant and submissive and to behave so as to please others. They are there to meet others' needs, wheras boys are there for themselves.* They also learn that misbehavior is not feminine. Boys *will* be boys, but girls *must* be girls. Home and school drill in the conviction; girls are passive, boys aggressive. Children's books reinforce the image in words and pictures:

> Girls, she discovers, are fearful, docile, foolish and sometimes downright stupid. Girls are dependent on other people—usually boys for motivation. Girls stand and watch while their brothers build scooters and race down the streets; they tag after their brothers and their brothers' friends but they can't quite keep up.**

---

*It is true that some boys are taught to care about others and meet their needs. These are the men who enter the "helping" professions—doctors, lawyers, teachers, ministers. But that is a kind of central concern for mankind. Such men are as aggressive in their achievement drives as any men. And in interpersonal relations with women they remain dominant.

**Betty Miles "Harmful Lessons Little Girls Learn in School," *Redbook,* March 1971, p. 167.

Girls are passive: passive is inferior: girls are inferior. Boys are aggressive: aggressive is superior: boys are superior. That is the awareness little girls begin to soak up from their earliest years. Parents often want sons first, or only sons if they can't have both. Boys are more valuable; they were never drowned in the Ganges. A little girl's letter to God is humorous at first, heartbreaking on reflection: "Dear God, are boys better than girls? I know you are one, but please be fair. Sylvia"*

Formal education perpetuates the deeply assimilated knowledge, just below awareness:

> From most books in use today, your daughter learns that because she is a girl, she is automatically inferior. "You're certainly not up to a man's work, so you'll start as a scrubwoman," one boy remarks. And other boys make statements such as "We men are the thinkers," and, "She is just like a girl—she gives up" without contradiction from adults or from girls themselves.
>
> The pictures portray more vividly than the few words of text that boys are vigorous and inventive, girls passive and indecisive. In one first grade reader a little girl, Sue, is allowed to choose a duck for a present. "Oh, my," says Sue. "Ducks and ducks and ducks. What will I do?" Up steps Jimmy to make the decision for her; the duck *he* chooses turns out to be just the one she wants.**

Taunts from my own childhood return to memory when I read something like that: "Stupid girl!" "You're only a girl!" (An early version of "only a woman"; "just a wife.") Have you ever heard "You're only a boy?" Boys are admonished to "Be a man!" Girls never hear "Be a woman!" It's "Be a big girl!" instead, meaning "Don't *really* grow up, just don't cause too much trouble." Language in general has a profound effect on what both girls and boys feel about themselves. It's hard to find yourself as a female in "man,"

---

*Eric Marshall and Stuart Hample, eds., *Children's Letters to God* (New York: Esandess, 1967).
**Miles, *op. cit.*, pp. 167–168.

"mankind," "he," "his." Small wonder that girls grow up feeling themselves a part of "The Woman Problem."

Of course, we don't make it easy for boys either. It's a heavy burden to have to be aggressive, superior, and successful in competitive ways all the time. Boys don't cry? Of course they do. They hurt and fear and despair as much as little girls do. But they are early taught to be brave, not to show it. Don't even feel it. Be a man! No wonder they have trouble getting at any feelings at all when they are grown. It is in these early years, too, that the overwhelming need to succeed is nurtured. Superiority must be maintained in a vicious and cutthroat world. Here's one man's view of his early programming:

> All these nasty little readers picture the boy as active, contentious, destructive, violent, thoughtless, wild, unsatisfied with the simple joys of the here and now, yearning, yearning, for new worlds to conquer. He's always wondering what he's going to be as a man. *He must be something.* He must achieve, he must triumph.*

Boys do feel. Most have to struggle with their own feelings of masculinity; many spend a lot of emotional energy striving not to be labeled unmanly. And girls *do* like action and adventure. Remember Nancy Drew? But a girl who takes leadership in an active way often is labeled unfeminine or unladylike! Things *are* changing somewhat. Increasingly I have the notion, and I think lots of other parents do too, that I hope my sons can be gentle as well as strong, and my daughter can be adventurous as well as sensitive, without the one being labeled sissy and the other tomboy.

Some signs of change are more dramatic:

> One woman, driving down the freeway with her husband, who is a doctor, in the back, heard their 5-year-old son say, "Daddies are doctors and mommies are nurses, right?" Mommy, a law student, writer and member of the neighborhood Women's

*Leo Haber, "Run, Dick, Run," *Saturday Review,* June 12, 1971.

Liberation cell, slammed on the brakes, turned around and shouted "Wrong!"

It was simple but, in the middle of the freeway, effective. Daddy and son, white-faced and shattered, came up in unison with "Daddies and mommies can both be doctors, right?" and the trip continued.*

A bit drastic perhaps, but a more and more common attitude as women begin to realize how little they liked the childhood programming that got them where they are.

Recently my daughter said to me, when I was carrying on about other people's stereotypes: "Mother, do you remember when I was small you told me not to lift the boys' weights because I'd get big muscles?" Did I ever say that? I can't believe it. I've changed. Little girls should lift weights if they want to!

A by-product of teaching girls that they are "naturally" submissive and inferior and boys that they are aggressive and superior is that both soon learn also that girls are "naturally dependent" and boys "naturally independent." A recent study illustrated that when a barrier is set up between toddlers and their mothers, little boys struggle to find a way out while little girls cry helplessly.** Girls have already learned by that age that the way to get what they want is to cry, and boys have learned that they will have to get what they want themselves. We do girls a tremendous disservice in this way. The importance of autonomy and separation from adults are built into the teaching, both conscious and unconscious, of boys. They are encouraged to develop a strong sense of independence and an identity of their own. But girls very quickly learn that their identity is dependent on relationships, and on an ability to manipulate and control people. Helpless crying is not as "helpless" as it sounds.

Our society begins in early years and in subtle ways to develop these sex-linked assignments. Parents and teachers help girls more than boys, reward girls for dependent behavior (Isn't she sweet) and

*Judith Martin, *Los Angeles Times,* November 1, 1971.
** *Time,* March 20, 1972, p. 44.

boys for independent behavior (Look how high he can climb). A now-famous line from a children's book, "Boys invent things. Girls use what boys invent,"* is another illustration. Culturally we do not encourage girls to be creative except biologically. There must be a lot of wasted female potential as a result of that attitude.

Of course these are general comments. Some girls do manage to be creative and independent in spite of the cultural brainwashing. Some boys do manage to develop a tender and gentle side. But I believe that almost all boys and girls experience the restrictions to some degree sooner or later.

As I think of the toddlers behind the barriers, I find that some of the old anger is still spooking around in me. I've been something like the little girl toddlers much of my life. For a long time a large part of me was content behind the barrier; there was plenty to do there as wife, mother, female. Then I began to want out. I cried, "Somebody get me out! Somebody help me!" Nobody came. Some of the time I blamed my husband, though he often encouraged me to get out. The helpless cry eventually became angry crying at those who, it seemed, had put me behind the barrier and were keeping me there. Much of the anger was justified. But neither the anger nor the crying got me out. Then I began struggling to get myself out. (This book is part of the struggle.) Many times it seemed easier to simply sit down and play behind the barrier, crying once in a while when I remembered that I really wanted out. But no more. A lot of the time I am out, and now I even enjoy the struggle much of the time.

We teach boys that they must be sufficient unto themselves, independent. We discourage girls from learning that. Both are hurt. Girls do not become independent enough. Boys become too independent —that is, they learn they must be the "strong, silent male" who doesn't need anyone else. The independent sense of self, of self-worth, must lie somewhere between what boys and girls learn. In the meet-me-in-the-middle philosophy there is a way to let children know that the *independent sense of self and the need for relation-*

Life, August 13, 1971, p. 55.

ships are not mutually exclusive! To be oneself and to need others go together. They are human needs, not sexual ones.

Besides limiting children in their capacity to be whatever they can be, such rigid programming deprives children of full and healthy relationships with adults of both sexes. If it's not fair or healthy for fathers to be denied closeness to their children, and it's not fair or healthy for mothers to be burdened with the whole responsibility for their physical and emotional care, it also isn't fair or healthy for children to get too much mother and not enough father, too many close female school teachers, and too many distant, usually punishing male school principals. Besides limiting their future choices by setting the example of what girls and boys can and cannot do when they grow up, it deprives them in childhood of close relationships with men in all areas of their lives; it loads them with guilt and the responsibility to be happy and successful so that their mothers will have been successful. The guilt that creates and perpetuates a national atonement rite like Mother's Day is spawned in childhood. "Momism" with all its destructive connotations is rooted in the knowledge early attained by the little girl that her only success in life, the only legitimate power she will ever have, is as a mother and through her children; and in the guilt of the little boy that makes him revere his mother, fear her power, and want to make up to her for his oppression of the entire feminine sex. That's where the domineering wife–henpecked husband relationship or the spoiled little boy–martyred mother marriage begins. Of course it's also rooted in the often too-strong clinging of mother to son, when a mother is frustrated by a lack of relationship with her husband and needs her son to take his place.

The discovery that the important thing is to be yourself first and a boy or girl second can be a truly freeing experience. I've seen the light dawn time and again in the play therapy room. What a relief to learn that girls can play with trucks and enjoy it! How great to find that boys can play with dolls and enjoy it! How satisfying to find that you are free to be and become. No more "Boys can't do that. Girls can't do this."

Won't children be confused? How will they know what a man is and what a woman is? Here we remind ourselves that males can be fathers and women can be mothers and that's the only absolute difference between them. It's enough! When parents aren't confused children won't be either. Meantime there will be confusion—for children and adults alike—as roles change faster, as more and more parents begin to change horses in midstream. Children old enough to have already internalized the stereotypes of what men are "supposed" to be and what women are "supposed" to be will certainly be confused and need help with assimilating the many changes. It's going to be some time before even five-year-olds don't have to question whether mommies can be doctors too. Many parents are unsure about what is really appropriate for men and women. So there is bound to be unsureness among children, too. That's the inevitable frustration of living during a time of rapid change.

Most of us, raised in our culture, have raised or are raising children who carry the burden of the old stereotypes. But it's never too late. As parents begin to change, children do too, and they in turn help to liberate their parents further. It's no use blaming ourselves for our mistakes with our children any more than it's any use blaming our parents for their mistakes with us. The answer is to start doing things differently.

As we move closer to the "different but equal" millennium, it will be as natural for children to grow into the kinds of inwardly liberated adults they see around them as it is to become like the models we now provide. We will not lose the tension between the sexes. Little girls and little boys will continue to go through the stages of loving each other and hating each other and fearing each other and being attracted to and needing each other. But these will be matters of individual sexual development rather than the outgrowth of a mutual need to keep men "masculine" by keeping women weak.

As a part of the growing sense of self and the growing capacity for relationship, liberated children must also be free to develop their own sexual identity as females or males. A sexually liberated child is one who learns early that the body and its impulses are good, that boys are just naturally boys and girls are just naturally girls physically and sexually, that there's a difference and the difference is very good! It means that boys and girls are free to be interested in and curious about their own bodies without overt or subtle disapproval from adults. It means that they can ask questions knowing they will be answered honestly. It means that sexual experimentation will be viewed as normal and will be handled openly and reasonably rather than with fear or shock or guilt. It means that children will find it easy and not difficult to learn about the body and sexual function of the sex which is not theirs.

How well I remember a birthday party when I was about five. One of the little boys left the bathroom door open when he went to urinate. Somehow I happened to pass by and stopped fascinated. It was something new, since I had no brothers. How I would have liked to go in and watch! But something told me that was wrong and I hurried along. I remember summertimes when we built tents of umbrellas and blankets in the back yard. We girls were interested in each other's bodies, too, and took such opportunities for innocent and harmless experimentation. I remember it so well now, not because of what we did, but because of the guilt that went along with it. And why did I have to ask a minister, at sixteen, whether kissing could make you pregnant? Surely I really knew the answer. But somehow the guilt about adolescent petting made me sure I would be punished. My parents never made specific prohibitions in these areas. And they gave me information when I needed it. But somehow I, and many other boys and girls, picked up the cultural attitude that sex was bad and wrong. Although it was less bad for boys, even they developed those attitudes. Masturbation, for example. We know now that that is a normal and even at times a desirable activity for both boys and girls.* Girls might enjoy sex more easily later on if they discovered earlier in life what feels good sexually.

*There are times when it is desirable for men and women too. It is a harmless and pleasurable way of releasing tension when more satisfying ways are impossible for some reason.

Neither the old repressive attitudes nor the new "anything goes" attitudes toward sex are any better for children than for adults. We must find a happy medium within which a child's sexual identity can grow as a concomitant both of the independent sense of self and the development of a human relationship. It is in the sexual realm that a child can develop a sense of her or his unique femaleness or maleness. Sex education that liberates children will emphasize the excitement of biological difference along with our mutual need for and joy in each other as female and male in all our "delightful diversity." The emphasis must be not on which is more valuable sexually but on how we can use our differentness to pleasure ourselves and each other. Since children learn these attitudes early in life, they must be part of our *feeling* as well as of our *formal* education of children.

So how do we grow liberated children? The obvious answer is that we must become more liberated adults. It's a circular motion. As parents and other adults begin to change, to relate to each other as equals, children will also become freer. Children raised by liberated parents in equalitarian marriages will be liberated themselves. Their inner freedom will make it possible for them to cope with the cultural boxes which change so slowly. Some people have already begun to put the circle in motion.

There are many steps we can take. Home and school are the most obvious and influential places to begin. As parents, we can make efforts to see that fathers as well as mothers are involved with their children. It seems to me that eventually we will require basic changes in our institutional structure to make this more easily possible. We will have to come to the point where as a society we see fathers having as much importance and responsibility in children's lives as mothers have always had. Part-time work for men, paternity leaves, willingness to hire both parents on a part-time basis if they are qualified—all these may have to become options in a society that makes a different assumption about sex roles than it now makes. As the need for productive work decreases and more leisure time is not only possible but mandatory for all, it will become easier for fathers as well as mothers to have more time with children.

Meantime, parents will have to go out of their way to provide time for family relationships on their own. More and more men are becoming disgusted with the competitive rat race, deciding it isn't worth it. They want more satisfying relationships with their children. That's a hopeful sign. One man we know, for example, moved to a new company that is pioneering with a four-day work week. He now has more time with his children, his wife has more freedom to pursue her interest in painting, and they both have more time together. A rising young bank executive withdrew from the country club golf circuit in order to have more time at home. He feels he may be risking his professional advancement somewhat, but he's decided it's worth it. He'll probably live longer, too!

It is apparently true that more and more couples are beginning to develop equalitarian relationships in which they are able to cross old sex lines more freely. That automatically brings fathers closer to their children. Whether or not both parents work outside the home, the parenting needs to be shared. The girl and the boy who see their father involved in parenting just as their mother is can see that as an option for themselves. The cultural myth that men are not biologically attuned to caring about children is destructive as well as inaccurate. When they get involved, fathers make as good mothers as mothers do! Sons who see their fathers being as concerned about parent-child relationships as they are about success on the job will themselves feel under far less pressure to "succeed" at the expense of heart attacks and ulcers, and will be far more ready to care about family life. The equalitarian relationship will be a *strengthening* one for families, not a weakening one as many people fear.

We need also to reform our educational system so that it no longer reinforces the stereotypes. That means changing everything from the materials used to the hiring practices. Books should picture fathers with aprons on and mothers as doctors, as well as vice versa.

One high school girl recently told her adult-living teacher about an experience she had as a kindergartner. When she pasted a picture of a man holding a baby on the page of her workbook entitled "Father's Jobs," the teacher marked this wrong—even though the girl explained she had seen her father holding a baby many times.*

These instances are beginning to change, though slowly. Organizations in several states are insisting on reevaluation of teaching materials and methods. We must also encourage men to become elementary teachers. More and more men are seeing this as important, but not enough. Women must be school principals in greater numbers too. Teachers, in other words, must be encouraged to do what they're good at, rather than what sex roles have dictated in the past. If you're great with elementary-age children, then teach them, even if you're a man. If you're a good administrator then be the school principal, even if you're a woman. You may have to fight for it! These abilities should be valued equally. Maybe someday we will find more realistic criteria for the way we pay people. The teacher is worth as much as the administrator. We couldn't have the school without either one.

Schools must also begin to put more emphasis on physical activities for girls and artistic and homemaking skills for boys. I'm not suggesting that everybody has to do everything together; but everyone should have a chance to try out everything without negative reaction from anyone. The kindergarten must find boys moving freely in and out of the doll and housekeeping corner and girls moving freely in and out of the truck and construction corner. The high school must provide as many sports opportunities for girls as it does for boys.

It is not only in sex role stereotyping that our education is too rigid. Many people, including educators, are beginning to raise questions about the effectiveness of our educational system. Some are saying we need to "deschool" the society**—that the rigid pattern on which education is based prevents learning rather than encourages it. The kind of humanizing education they are talking about is possible in a setting that encourages every individual to do and learn

*Gail McClure, et al., *Today's Education,* November 1971, p. 33.
**Ivan Illich, *Deschooling Society* (New York: Harper & Row, 1971).

whatever he or she can do and learn. That kind of education can liberate children to become fully human according to their individual potential.

A lot is being said these days about the isolation of the nuclear family. It is true that much burden has been placed on mother, father, and children to be sufficient unto themselves. It is also much easier to emphasize the role division in a nuclear family—things run more smoothly if there's no question about who does what—as long as everyone is happy with what he or she does. The extended family of the past is not likely to return, at least not in the forseeable future. One of the best things that can happen to children, and to their parents, too, is for the family to *create* an extended family. Time was when several generations of relatives lived together so that there were a number of children and a number of adults for them to relate to. Though that often meant serious problems, chiefly in the neurotic involvement of too many relatives in each other's lives, there were some advantages too. Children were not so dependent on their own parents for all their nurturing satisfactions, for all their care, for all their adult models. Parents were not so burdened by the full-time responsibility for their children. Each could get away from the other for periods of time. Children had a number of models of maleness and femaleness, though they were rigid models. And there were people of many ages and several generations for children to relate to.

Although institutions, especially schools, have taken up some of these functions, by and large the nuclear family is dependent on itself for nurturing and caretaking functions. Hence the need for an artifically created extended family. It can have the advantages without the disadvantages of the old way. Some people are taking steps in this direction. A group of several families may spend a good deal of time together, though they live in separate houses. When our children were little, several families we knew used to spend frequent weekend and summer camping trips together. As the men got older and busier and the children got older and less interested, it petered out. But it was a good idea; I think we would work harder at it now, aware as we are of the importance of other people to us and to our children.

An increasing number of families are deciding to develop some kind of communal living arrangement, as discussed earlier in the book. In such an arrangement, children automatically develop an image of the variety of roles and tasks that both men and women can engage in. Children have a number of adults to whom to turn in any situation and can learn to trust not just two, but several, adults.

The physical setting in which children are raised is not nearly as important as the emotional health of the persons with whom they have regular relationships. Day-care centers are options for working parents if they are staffed with the same warm, healthy, nurturing, secure *men* and women over a period of time, so that relationships of intimacy are possible. From time to time some one, usually a medical *man,* makes the pronouncement that a child needs the constant attention of the mother for the first ten months or two years or whatever for some deep biological reason. There is simply no evidence to support that. A child needs the *same* loving one or two or three mothering-fathering *persons,* male or female, yes, but not necessarily its natural mother. Adoptive children are certainly ample evidence of that. But day-care centers are only a partial answer. They can be helpful, but it is not fair either to parents or to children to make that the only answer. Certainly children should never be "dumped" in any old day-care center. Single parents are often victims of such an attitude. Forcing unwed mothers to work contradicts our public policy about children needing their parents. As a society we need to sanction a number of settings in which children can have the consistent loving care of a small number of adults over a long period in their early years, without depriving half the population—women—of the opportunity for other kinds of fulfillment too. We will have to change both our attitudes and our practices *drastically* to achieve that.

How to free children to develop an independent sense of self and a capacity for deeply feeling relationships is both an individual and a cultural matter. They must be freed from the tightly binding sexual stereotypes of what is a boy and what is a girl. They must be freed from distant fathers and trapped mothers. We can do many things to help our children become full human beings. We can give little boys dolls and doll houses and little girls construction sets and doctor equipment. We can take girls to the fire house and boys to the dance concert, if they want to go. We can insist that schools examine both their methods and their materials. We can buy the kind of books for our children that do not perpetuate old stereotypes. Many are now available. Sunday school and church teaching is often the most offensive of all. Parents can have lots of influence in insisting that church school literature be changed. Parents can provide at home, and insist on schools and churches providing, the kind of sex education that makes accurate information available in a context of warmth and respect for both sexes.

A number of organizations and movements across the country have begun to cry for the liberation of children. One emphasis is on the need to protect children from physical abuse in homes and schools. Others are exploring new ideas to free children to learn more effectively. Some groups emphasize the right of children to be raised by parents or adults who can provide an atmosphere of emotional health. The issue of the rights of parents if they conflict with the rights of children is being raised anew. Many groups are concerned with the right of children to grow up free from poverty, free from ignorance, free from prejudice. Freedom from the constriction of rigid role stereotypes is one of many aspects of children's liberation, of human liberation. Children must be free to be and become whatever they can be and become. And that means they must be warm and well fed, well clothed and housed, and grow up in families and societies that make it possible for them to grow to their full stature, female or male. "The best thing we adults could do for children would be to renovate our institutions and give the young a livable world to grow up in."* Children are more than "sugar and spice and everything nice" or "snakes and snails and puppy dogs'

*Paul Goodman, *Children's Rights* (New York: Praeger Publishers, 1971), p. 8.

tails.'' They are young human beings who need and have the right to grow up in a nurturing society that affirms their humanity and provides them with whatever options make it most possible for them to become fully human, whatever their sex.

Seven / Liberated Work

When I went back to school several years ago, it was in the firm conviction that the only way for a woman to replace the loss of motherhood as a full-time job was with a career. My sister says that I joined the Menopausal Masters association! I think she's right. If I were making the decision again, I would make the same one, I suspect, because it has turned out well for me. But I no longer believe that it was the only possible choice. There are so many ways for a woman to go now, so many directions I might take, or might have taken. There ought to be, and increasingly there are, many options for a woman at any stage of life, options that can be both satisfying to her and worthwhile for society. The same must be said for men. For although the hue and cry now is over woman's work—can she be satisfied at home or must she get out of the home?—it is also true that many men are dissatisfied and unfulfilled in the work they have chosen or drifted into. Many middle-aged men, especially, feel as trapped vocationally as the much-discussed "trapped housewife." Many young men are finding that the old "work ethic" doesn't fit, but society hasn't many answers yet to what the new ways can be.

It is time to develop a society in which both women and men can be involved in "liberated work." That means that every person must have the freedom to do the kind of work he or she wants to do, that uses his or her gifts fully, and that serves some constructive purpose in society. Liberated work is liberating work. It is humanizing work. It requires new definitions of "work" that will allow all of us to share the world's "dirty work" as well as the kinds of work that are satisfying. And it means that we must define work as whatever improves our chances for surviving on this planet as well as in ways that allow every individual to reach his or her fullest humanness. Work can no longer mean simply "getting things done" or producing "things for a better life." That sounds unrealistic, particularly when I think of the millions of people whose present work is satisfying only for the money it brings to keep them alive or to have more and better things. But it is a goal which we can—must—work toward.

Our remarkable diversity and intelligence as human beings suggest that we have hardly begun to tap our creative resources. Humanity has used much of its energy so far in figuring out ways to subdue the planet and each other. Besides that, in our single-minded efforts to divide up work into "masculine" and "feminine" categories, we've deprived both sexes of infinite individual opportunities and humanity of the benefits of untold creativity. For either sex, not to fit is to fail. We need to change that now, not just for women but for our survival.

But I was speaking of my own choice to return to school so that I could prepare myself to enter the "male world" of achievement and success. I believe now that just as I marched into motherhood in my early life without much conscious thought, I also prodded myself into a career in middle age without considering whether there were other options. And—in both instances, I am now aware—I could have considered what those other choices were. I'm lucky that my blind choices turned out well. But many women are making similar choices now because it seems the thing to do, and then finding it isn't for them at all.

Why does a career, for many middle-aged women, seem like the only choice? I think for the same reason that wifing and motherhood often seems the only choice for younger women. Those are the accepted values of society. As young women we automatically choose motherhood first because that's what society says is the way to be a woman. When motherhood is over, we choose a career— usually a "feminine" one—teaching or social work or nursing. Society says that success and achievement in a career are more valuable than volunteer work, for example. So many of us go in that direction, even though it may or may not be right for us individually or for society.

The "woman question" is complicated. Oversimplified answers turn out not to be answers at all. Many women are saying that the traditional roles for women are no longer good, that modern women really can't fulfill themselves in this way. These women are sincere in that feeling. For them it has *not* been satisfying. The mistake comes when we try to impose the same judgment on all women. For many women the traditional roles *are* satisfying. They desire no other. And for still another group of women they are partially satisfying but need supplementing with other kinds of activity and commitment, either concurrently or subsequently. Some women believe they are satisfied but are troubled by amorphous and ill-defined feelings of discontent, tension, or frustration.

Consider the following statements. The first is from a Letter to the Editor responding to an article on women's liberation: "Be a lawyer, doctor, truck driver or piano tuner if you want to be, but don't make me, however subtly, feel less a human being because I choose to be a wife, mother and homemaker."* The second is from a newspaper article: "OK. So I'm not a women's libber. I love my husband. I love my kids, and I wanted to be with them full time when they were small. But while I was home, the longer I stayed there the more the doors kept closing, preventing me from ever going back to what I once had. In today's society is that the price a woman must pay?"**

The first woman feels people are telling her she's no good because she is happy to be housewife and mother. But why does it bother her that some women are saying she isn't really fulfilling herself at home? Why is it hard to let it be "their problem"? It's because as a culture we have *not* valued women and women's work, so she herself isn't sure that what she's choosing to do *is* important.

The second woman has other frustrations. She is feeling good about her mothering days, now coming to an end. And she wants to get into something else, but finds the job market glutted except with busy-work jobs or jobs for which her skills are obsolete.

Redbook, April 1972, p. 4.
**Joan Wixen, *Los Angeles Times,* September 14, 1972.

". . . these are the lucky ones, the ones without this inner turmoil. This turmoil that some of us have that gnaws away and tears us up inside because we feel that we're a nobody unless we do something. Something that says you're using your creative ability to the fullest and you're getting paid for it."*

It's a sad situation when we are valued as human beings in our society chiefly for what we do and how much we get paid for it. What is the answer? Must everyone, women as well as men, find a job or career that is both creative and pays well? Impossible! There are neither enough jobs nor a need for them. The answer is in changing our system of values, and that will take time. But it must come if we are to achieve genuine human liberation.

Take housework. There is no doubt that being a full-time wife, mother, and homemaker has many and deep satisfactions for many women. But, let's face it, the major satisfactions simply are not in keeping the toilet clean, or even in the endless stacks of freshly folded towels that give momentary pleasure. The major rewards in the traditional woman's role are in the relationships, both for their own sakes and for the sense of success one feels as wife and mother when children turn out well, when one's creative abilities make husband and children happy, when one feels rewarded by family and friends because one *is* a good wife and mother. When children are small, these satisfactions *can* be consuming for many women. (They could be for men, too, if that were part of the masculine role. And it ought to be a live option.) Nonetheless, most women feel one down when they choose these roles, *even if they are satisfying.* Homemaking is not one of society's most respected careers. If you doubt that, consider the following:

> How many men—and women themselves—fall into that mental trap? "My wife doesn't work," the businessman tells his friends. "Are you working, or are you a housewife?" the traffic cop asks the woman he stops for speeding. "I'm not working. I'm just a housewife," murmur countless women in reply to an occupa-

* *Ibid.*

tional question. One woman became so accustomed to deni-
grating her daily toil that, when asked "What do you do?" she
found herself answering, "My husband's an engineer."*

One dictionary defines "housewife" as "one who does not work
for a living." Yet the average woman with children at home works
at her job of nursemaid-buyer-cook-dishwasher-housekeeper-
chauffeur-laundress-seamstress-practical nurse-maintenance man-
gardener-teacher-counselor at least 99.6 hours a week. If she were
hired on the open market and paid at current rates, she'd make
$257.53 a week—that's a national average. It's more in some states,
less in others. But she's not a "working woman." She's "just a
housewife," one who doesn't work for a living. Some of us try to
upgrade our image in our own and other people's eyes by calling
ourselves "homemakers." Another dictionary defines homemakers
thus: "a person who manages a home, as a housewife or
housekeeper." Well, that didn't get us very far up the ladder, did it?

For whatever reasons, and there are many—because we're
women, because housewifing requires no training, keeps no formal
hours, has no formal standards to meet (except "she's a lousy
housekeeper," or, when children misbehave, "she must be a terrible
mother")—society devalues housewifing, and so, however much we
protest otherwise, we women devalue it too. We don't think of it as
really important. It's no wonder we "feel less than human" and on
the defensive when other women come along and tell us to get out
of the home.

The words housewife and homemaker do not really describe the
most rewarding part of the traditional woman's role—motherhood.
In the children's early months and years a woman can find herself
fulfilled and with a sense of power and achievement as she relates
to small beings who need her and respond to her with warmth and
joy and dependence. But the children grow up. A job of mothering
well done is soon no longer a job. And even while it is fully consum-

---

*This quote and many of the facts in this section are from Ann Crittendon Scott,
"The Value of Housework," *Ms,* July 1972.

ing many women have ambivalent feelings about it. Our mistake as a culture has been not in saying that women are mothers, but in saying that that is all they *can* be. So when the diapers and the dirty faces and the whiny voices become just too much many women feel guilty, tempted as they often are by thoughts of some other kind of life—of taking piano lessons themselves, or of working part time, or of going into politics, or of reading a book even. Some women apparently still whisk the magazine under the pillow, literally or figuratively, when husband or society are looking. Recently after a discussion with a group of young mothers in which we had shared some of the frustrations of homemaking, I received a letter that contained this line: "Many guilt feelings left me that morning and I will be more responsive to what I really think is 'my thing' instead of being pushed into many activities because as a woman I feel I should be doing them."* What is needed for "homemaking" to be liberated is neither a glorification of motherhood (sometime take a poll of the women you know: "How do you feel about Mother's Day?") nor a denigration of housewifing. What *is* needed is a realistic assessment of which parts of women's traditional role are valuable and satisfying, like the mothering relationship and the wife-husband intimacy, and the creative and artistic aspects; which parts are necessary but not very satisfying, like cleaning the bathroom and waxing the floor; and which parts are neither satisfying nor necessary, like being a perfect housekeeper. Then we can value the first, reward the second, and eliminate the third.

The worldwide need for population control means that a family can average no more than two children, probably for some generations to come if we are to avoid widespread famine and a drastic reduction in the quality of life. So the woman who chooses to stay home while her children are small needs to be planning what she will do for the forty years of her life after that. On the other hand, there are millions of children all over the world who need homes. Surely there is some way to break down both the psychological and the

---

*Lines from a letter from Carol Johnson.

international political barriers so that those children could be adopted into homes that want them. A single or married woman (or a man) who wants to make a vocation of motherhood could do so under those circumstances.

If a woman finds that she wants to do something else instead of or besides motherhood or when motherhood is over, she ought to be free to do what she decides is interesting and worthwhile. Unfortunately, society makes women feel inferior if they do not choose occupations that are rewarded with money and prestige. If you add up all the volunteer work that women do—fund-raising for worthy causes, political action, social service, church work, tutoring, chauffering sick children to hospitals, and many, many others—the time, energy, and volume of worthwhile work accomplished must be tremendous. Still, how many condescending remarks and jokes do you hear about "do-gooders," women who spend much of their time in volunteer work. No doubt some of it is a waste of time. Not most of it. But because it's women's work, it's not very valuable. Certainly not essential. Men who do volunteer work often get lots of praise; they are considered to be sacrificing time from their important work. But women "don't have anything else to do anyway. It keeps them busy. Keeps them out of trouble." That's what I heard a man say recently about the League of Women Voters, which does a remarkably important and valuable job.

A friend of mine made the remark that maybe one reason we don't really get busy and feed the hungry—eliminate poverty—is that the poor have always been woman's work.* No doubt that's just one reason. But it's true that we do not as a society value the nurturing concerns as we do the competitive ones.

All of which probably explains the unconscious factors in my choice of a remunerative career instead of a volunteer one. But the latter might have been an option for me. As a woman I need no longer swallow the cultural propaganda that what I am and what I do aren't important. As more and more women begin to feel

*Patricia Doyle, "Comments on Liberation and Survival."

"whole," the value of women, of motherhood, of volunteer work will go up. Volunteer work has always reflected the nurturing side of human personality—and that's traditionally female. When we do value it as a society, men will also get involved and we will begin to have peace and an end to poverty. The option that many women choose, to become deeply involved in worthwhile volunteerism, needs to be recognized for the important work it is.

It is also true, of course, that 28 million American women work outside the home. At first glance it appears that many women are "fulfilling" themselves in other ways than homemaking. But two-thirds of these working women are in low-income jobs, working because they must, not because they want to, and often raising children and doing housework as well. The percentage of professional women—those whom we could assume are really fulfilled in their work—decreased between 1940 and 1970. Menial jobs, low pay, and no opportunity for advancement are the lot of many women who have jobs away from home.

Margaret Mead* points out that every known human society has recognized the male's need for achievement at the expense of women. There have always been role differentiations, and whatever jobs have been assigned to the male have been the important jobs. If cooking or weaving were done by the men, then cooking or weaving were the important tasks in the culture. The same jobs, when they were assigned to women, immediately became less important. She feels that in most cultures male achievement is based on achieving something that women cannot do, or cannot do well. In other words, woman must be unimportant in order for man to be important. We became aware of that when we were in Russia; 86 percent of the doctors are women, but medicine is not a prestige profession.

It is not that all men are happily fulfilled in their work and all women are not. Too many men are also underpaid and doing work

---

*Margaret Mead, *Male and Female* (New York: William Morrow & Co., 1949), p. 159.

that is degrading or unsatisfying or devalued by society. The only advantage such men have is that they may be "king of the castle" at home.

As a culture we have been concerned for some time about the high incidence of heart attack and the lower life expectancy of men, who are forced into a competitive and achievement-oriented society. But no one until now has begun to view with alarm the fact that half the human race has had to fit into one role that has been assumed to be "right" for all women. We need now to *urge* women to participate in the world outside the home as well as in it for their own sakes as well as for humanity's sake. We do society a disservice if we continue to see that woman's primary place is in the home. And it is unrealistic to think that we can continue to educate women in the same way we do men to want and be able to participate in the larger society, and then prevent them from doing it.

Does that mean that every woman should go out and get a job? No. It does mean that every woman should develop some sense of responsibility for the way the world is going, and stop leaving it to, and blaming it on, men. For if we are honest we have to admit that as women we are sometimes comfortable in our dependence, as well as impatient with it. It's easier to play bridge and sleep late. But it won't do. If we are asking men to meet us in the middle then we have to take more responsibility than we have taken in the past for what goes on outside our homes in the world we send our children into.

It may be that the revolution in women's roles will bring us to the place where we can meet in the middle, where we can share our talents and our abilities, whatever they are, and not according to what is permitted for our sex. As women begin to insist on taking their share of the load and to demand their share of the satisfaction of making the world go round, men can gain some of the good things that women have always had—more time with their children, more time for relationships of all kinds. Maybe as women get to know themselves and each other better, men will begin to benefit; maybe men, too, can learn to talk to each other, to reject the "masculine mystique," to question the rules of society that keep them from feelings, from relationships, from living out their lives without the threat of early death. It's happening. More and more men are beginning to question their success-at-any-price goals, their current satisfactions, and to ask whether some other life-style might be better. Lots of men feel pushed and pressured into the frantic scramble for success by the women in their lives, which is another reason that the freeing of women to be full human beings will free men too.

Sometimes in the earlier years of my housekeeping, particularly as I began to be more "liberated," I used to complain to Howard about the drudgery of housekeeping. He usually said something like "Well, my work has drudgery, too." So we argued about whose job had the most unpleasant requirements. (He admits that I could win that one hands down.) Certainly every job has its drudgery. Some have more than others. Housekeeping is high on the list of drudge jobs. But let's be fair. In some ways the middle-aged, affluent, middle-class American male is less free than his wife. I can decide, have decided, that the old way is not for me. I can go back to school, work part time or full time or not at all, spend all my time writing, grow flowers, go into politics, whatever I like, now that my children are grown and my husband is a success. I can sit and do nothing if I like, and society will say it's okay. But Howard doesn't have those options. Lots of men are feeling just as dissatisfied and unfulfilled as lots of women are. Most do not have the option to change, either in the form of a mandate from society or as a financial possibility. A successful man who suddenly wants to do his thing is effectively trapped. For one thing, his wife couldn't support him, in most cases. Though there may be more satisfaction for more men in the kinds of work they have chosen, they are more trapped by their choices than women are. As roles begin to blend, as women begin to take as much responsibility as men for the financial status of the family, inevitably men will gain more of that kind of freedom too.

I have to keep reminding myself that when I talk of options for either sex, I'm talking about reasonably affluent Americans. It's obvious that there are millions of people even in this country, both men and women, who endure lives of drudgery, with little work satisfaction and no choices or options for anything better. That too is an inevitable result of our money and production economy. We value things more than people, and therefore we value what people can do—how productive they can be—more than we value people themselves. How can we change that?

The time has come when we not only don't *need* more material things, but our very survival on the planet depends on conserving and replacing our natural resources. We cannot go on creating more jobs to make more things to be used by more people. There are, of course, some new directions we can take that will provide plenty of jobs for a long time to come—preserving the environment, eliminating disease, exploring space, for example. But even if we phase out work that is destructive to human survival—war industries, the pollution of the planet—and phase in new kinds of work that will help us to save humanity and raise it to higher levels, there still will not be enough remunerative work indefinitely for everyone.

We are faced with not only the opportunity but the responsibility to develop new, more satisfying ways to use our time, both in creative work and in play. We need basic changes in the way our society is organized, some alternatives to 8-hour days and 40-hour weeks. Already some of that is happening—3-day weeks, 4-hour days, for instance. That means basic changes in what we value. No longer can money and production be our chief gods. We will have to value other kinds of creativity and achievement. We need to rediscover that it is valuable to lie on the grass and gaze at the sky, to sit and think, to read for the sake of knowledge and pleasure, to investigate the 90 percent of our human potential that we know nothing about. We must rediscover the arts. How about another Renaissance? We must put more of our energies into the study of disease and of human relationships so that our understanding of ourselves catches up with our remarkable technological achievements. There seems no longer any excuse for a world full of war, misery, poverty, and affluent meaninglessness when we so obviously have the hearts and the minds to discover how to be human together.

We must try new ways of organizing the world of work so that it is a part of, not separate from, other aspects of life. We need to divide up the routine functions and the creative ones so that everyone gets some of each. Shouldn't we stop labeling some jobs as more important than others and start valuing every person's contribution to society equally—both in money and prestige? That sounds utopian but it is not unrealistic. I am as dependent on the plumber and the garbage collector and the farmer as I am on the mayor and the bank president and the doctor. None of us could exist without the others. The kind of work we do should not determine our status or our standard of living. A friend of mine made an interesting statement in that connection: "I'm not sure that drudgery deserves its bad name. I think more of us need to be closer to our basic needs and functions. The drudgery mind-set seems to be supportive of the caste (mistress-maid, master-servant) system. Maybe cleaning up after yourself deserves elevated social status."* If we choose not to take care of our own individual basic needs, then we need to change our attitudes toward the people who do. If I want to have my house cleaned by someone else, then I need to respect the person who does it and pay well for the job. Or maybe the people who do the most unpleasant work ought to be the most highly paid. Certainly we ought to equalize and stablize incomes on the basis of the value of persons. That's the only way to end poverty.

A new approach to work will mean we must reassess our use of leisure time. We need to subsidize the arts and make it possible for all who have the interest and talent to participate, not just those few who have the leisure and the money. We need to discover how to have fun in nondestructive ways that are not simply methods of "killing time," or of getting new "thrills," or of finding reality-deadening escapes. In order to find ways to reach these goals, to make the basic changes our society needs, to discover ways to avoid mass suicide, we will have to use all the creative people we've got. Studies indicate that the most creative people are those who are able to use

*Rachel Roy, "Comments on Liberated Work." Unpublished paper October 28, 1972.

easily both the traditionally "feminine" and the traditionally "masculine" sides of their personalities. Creative people are high in independent judgment, ambition, and other so-called "masculine" traits. They are also high in sensitivity, perceptiveness, and other so-called "feminine" traits. If our most creative individuals are such whole people, doesn't it also make sense that collectively we would be more creative if we encouraged in both women and men the full use of the qualities we have traditionally divided between the sexes?

While I've been working on this chapter an old hymn from my childhood has been singing itself in my head: "Work for the night is coming. . . ." The song has chiefly nostalgic meaning for me now, though if I redefine both "work" and "night" it still has other meaning, too. Work in the old sense of "getting things done" and "don't waste time" is too narrow a conception. Liberated work is more even than being free as individuals to do whatever we want to do and can do. It isn't enough that a few of the world's peoples—affluent middle- and upper-class women and men—are free to fulfill themselves. Liberated work is a sharing along human lines, not sex, or race or class lines, of all that *needs* to be done for our emotional and physical well-being, all that *can* be done for our aesthetic and intellectual satisfaction, and all that *must* be done to free all women and men everywhere to reach their own highest human and spiritual potential. We need to stop creating *things* and start recreating *each other*. And that will take all of us, of all ages, colors, and sexes, working together.

Eight / Sexism and Survival

Often these days I am accused with some validity of having a one-track mind. Because I feel so strongly about equality for women, I have trouble keeping the issue in perspective. I tend to bring all issues back to that one. Women's liberation is one of a number of vital social concerns along with racial equality, the elimination of poverty, peace, the restoration of the environment, the need to control over-population. All of these issues are intricately interwoven and inter-dependent, and must be attacked simultaneously. At the same time I believe objectively that the equality of the sexes is *basic* to all the others. Not that we can wait to work on the other things until equality of the sexes has become a reality. There are no firsts among these issues. At the same time, however, the equality of women and men is so closely bound up with human survival that it's simply no use even talking about the one without the other! Until we esteem women equally with men we will not revere the traditional "feminine" qualities of nurturing and caring—the humanitarian values the culture mouths but does not implement. These have been labeled "feminine," therefore "weak," all over the world. The dominant culture holds that it is more important to subdue the world's peoples than to feed them. But we don't need any more guns and bombs. The rape of the environment must stop or we will all die. What we need now is to feed and clothe the poor, to provide adequate health care for everyone, to nurture human life everywhere, to preserve and re-create the environment. Until the "feminine" values become hu-man values, the world will not turn from its destructive course. A genuine respect for the traditionally feminine value of nurturing in men as well as in women will hasten the equality of women. Conversely, the valuing of women equally with men will hasten the valuing of nurturing and caring. We can't have one without the other.

So I believe there is some justification for my one-track mind, and for my anger when someone says something like, "Well, of course I believe in equal pay for equal work and all that, but most of what women complain about seems so petty. The real issues are war and poverty and human survival. Women ought to forget about their own little problems and start concentrating on the important ones." Some of my most intelligent male friends, though they are kind enough not to put it in words, quite obviously feel that way. When I wax eloquent about the importance of equality for women if the human race is to survive, they smile superciliously and hurry on to their concerns about war and poverty and human survival.

I used to do a slow burn or even a boil when I felt thus patronized. It still bothers me, but now I just shrug my shoulders and try to get on with it. Or sometimes when I am hurt and angry, it helps to tell myself some female chauvinist jokes! Like the cartoon that shows two very civilized-looking young cavewomen watching the approach of a great apelike oaf of a caveman. One woman is saying to the other, "Oh my gosh! Now they too can walk upright!" Or the graffiti line, "Women who seek to be equal with men lack ambition!" Anyway, having drained off my anger, I can, as I say, get on with it.

Certainly it is true that in countries like the United States where we are generally well fed, we can think about human rights. It's no accident that the movement for women's liberation has found its most fertile soil among educated, affluent middle-class women. "I'm not trying to speak of other places. I wouldn't dare. What could I say about men and women in India? Food has all the authority in starvation. Sexual politics and sexual opinions, and I suppose sexuality itself, are all fringe benefits of eating."*True. At the same time those of us who have enough to eat have the option and the responsibility to discover new ways of doing things. We can't wait until every one is fed to start talking about equality for women or any other group.

*Mary Ellman, *Thinking About Women* (New York: Harcourt Brace, 1968), p. xv.

Especially when it begins to look as though our present approach is certainly not getting everybody fed, much less equal. That's why it's impossible to separate sexual equality from human survival.

The current flowering of the women's rights movement grew out of the civil rights and student activist movement of the fifties and sixties in which many young women and men all over the country were involved. All too often women found themselves making coffee and stuffing envelopes instead of planning strategy and taking action. And when they complained or insisted on being involved in other ways they were promptly "put in their place." As though it were possible to have racial equality without sexual equality or vice versa. All equalities are mutually interdependent—all *people* are created equal.

A fascinating article about the United Nations appeared in the newspaper recently. The U.N. is probably the greatest humanitarian body in the world. Its charter asserts its dedication to the principle of equal rights and self-determination for all peoples. Yet, as is true of all the institutions of society, women therein remain second-class citizens. The article quotes women employees who say that the U.N. treats them, both in attitude and in pay and promotion, by standards that do not uphold its charter. The most telling remarks are the following:

> The aroused women are employees—those who work as international civil servants in the huge UN bureaucracy here and around the world, doing the paper work and research for the 132 national delegations which meet to debate and vote.
>
> Most countries include one or more women in their delegations to the General Assembly each fall, but the UN women do not expect much help from them. Women delegates usually are assigned by their governments to the social, humanitarian and cultural committee—the "ladies committee" of the seven main assembly bodies and *one of the least influential* (italics mine).*

Just the words "ladies committee" illustrate the amused contempt in which that committee is held. Something to keep the ladies busy. Do

Los Angeles Times, June 7, 1972.

we assign women to the social, humanitarian, and cultural commit-tee because we don't think those *issues* are important, or because *women* aren't important? Both.

The major nurturing movement afoot these days, led mostly by men because they have the training and the expertise required, is the ecology movement. Like men in the church, these are unusual men who are willing to value their "feminine" side—the nurturing, caring, preserving, creating qualities. But so far they are not listened to by large segments of society. They are considered by many to be doom-sayers, pessimists, anti–technologists. The values that ecologists es-pouse, the "feminine" values, are secondary. Until we raise the status of women, until we value the "feminine" in us all, we fight a losing battle to preserve the planet.

The world society reveres those organizations and activities that represent or carry out characteristics of the dominant male culture. Thus the United Nations, a humanitarian, peace-keeping organiza-tion, has little prestige and less power compared to the world's great military complexes. The United States has a huge foreign aid budget, but the overwhelming proportion of it is in military rather than hu-manitarian aid. Although many people, including many men, are interested in and concerned about poverty and ecology and peace, these issues get the least time and attention and money all over the world. And not only because of men. Most women also feel that power and dominance are more valuable than nurturing and caring. They do not value the "feminine" characteristics any more than most men do. How will we learn that these are not feminine but human characteristics, and essential to our survival?

As we visit various countries around the world, Howard and I have been interested to notice the kinds of things people everywhere build monuments to, especially the statues of people. Overwhelmingly the predominant themes are military—the conquering hero images: men in armor, men on charging horses, men who commanded great ships or navies, men who came home victorious from war. Some great cities have dozens of such statues. Washington, D.C., is one huge monument to military prowess. Only rarely are there statues of artists or musicians; we were glad to find Mozart and Beethoven and

Brahms in Germany, and here and there Goethe or Nietzsche. New England has enshrined some of its famous nineteenth-century authors. But these are the exceptions. Even statues of great statesmen are usually those who led their countries safely through war—Lincoln, for example, and Churchill. Most of the world's heroes are victorious, conquering males, soldiers or kings. There are some statues of religious leaders, especially in Europe—usually the militant ones, though their causes were often humane. As to women, there are a few queens here and there, and other noble women, most of whom led in some humanitarian cause—Florence Nightingale is one. And there are lots of statues of female nudes everywhere—monuments to the beauty of the female body—and a few beautiful male bodies, too. But generally the people we enshrine publicly represent the values of dominance that we enshrine internally.

Endless war, nuclear weapons that can destroy humankind, decaying cities, racial and religious discrimination, pollution, and all the rest are the results of having for centuries exalted dominance, power, and victory.

It won't work any more, not for the people and not for the planet. There can be no statue for the person who presses the button that sets off the nuclear holocaust, or to the subduers of the environment who use up the natural resources and pollute the air and water. The masculine-feminine dichotomy is obsolete. *In arbitrarily assigning two different sets of acceptable traits and, therefore, roles to women and men, and in assigning lower value to the female ones, we have denigrated a whole range of characteristics necessary for survival.*

What *will* happen as more and more women move into politics and other arenas of public life? What will happen when there are 50 female senators and 50 male ones instead of 100 men and no women? And 218 women representatives and the same number of men instead of 420 and 16? It's an interesting thought. Will they bring with them compassion and caring, nurturing and love, or will they simply become "like men"? Won't women be just as belligerent and conquering and power-mad as men? Won't they be just as eager to drop bombs and fire missiles and build arsenals? Certainly it is true that women have a violent side. Some of the anger the world is hearing from women these days is related to the growing consciousness of women's oppressed role in society. That anger will dissipate as women become more equal. But probably we cannot assume that the mere fact of women moving into public life will mean a dramatic change in attitudes. Some of women's angry, aggressive side is simply human. Add to that the fact that women have internalized the dominant values of the culture—they too feel that power and dominance are superior values—and it becomes obvious that compassion and caring will not automatically take over when women are equally represented in politics or government. Women have been called "the real haters."* Television pictures of affluent white women spitting on small black schoolchildren give credence to the accusation. But such incidents may represent both individual pathology and the perverted use of power that results when legitimate uses are frustrated. Besides, it has been true up until now, and still is to some degree, that women who "make it" in public life have to become "like men"—that is, in order to succeed they have to adopt the aggressive, competitive, domineering tactics of success.

But I am continually drawn back to my main thesis: that as women become more and more involved in public life, they will become more highly valued and that therefore the traits traditionally labeled "feminine" will also become valued in both sexes. A recent study** indicated that a majority of people believe that "women are more sensitive to the problems of the poor and underprivileged than men are" and that they attach a greater value to human life. But these are simply the things women have been trained to care about. Many men hold those values too, and as they become "human" rather than "feminine" values they will be more influential. If sensitivity to others and the nurturing of life were considered the strong, important values instead of the weak, "feminine" ones, the saturation bombing of Vietnam and other atrocities could not happen.

As more women move into public life they will be able to use their

---

*Richard M. Nixon, speech quoted in *Ms.,* July 1972, p. 47.
**Virginia Slims–Harris Setlow Poll, *Los Angeles Times,* March 24, 1972.

strong sides in "caring" ways. That will release more men to use their nurturing sides too. There will be a gradual change in values toward a more human balance between the gentle and the aggressive. What the world needs these days is some pretty *aggressive caring.*

Women are only now beginning to examine themselves both individually and collectively as human beings who are women, in some ways different from men, but in most ways like them. Old assumptions about women in public life, that they are "masculinized," though that may have been true in the past, are now being examined and questioned. Women are just beginning to look at themselves and their potential as a political and social force not dependent on what men think. It has been assumed with some validity by women as well as men over the years that women vote like their fathers or their husbands, that women are more conservative than men, that they vote for the most sexually attractive man, that they accept politics as right for men but not for women. Women who are interested in politics join the League of Women Voters; men who are interested in politics run for office.

The old ways of women in public life have less validity now and will continue to have even less as increasing numbers of women take a vigorous role in public life. An interesting finding in the study already mentioned* was that fewer women than has been supposed vote like their husbands, though many husbands thought they did. Women are beginning to speak with an independent voice.

It is difficult for us as women to overcome the old programming. Though we have had the vote in this country for fifty years, and though there are eight million more eligible female voters than men, up to now fewer votes are actually cast by women. Although more and more women believe in equal rights for women and in the importance of involving women in politics, most are still waiting for other women to take up the cause for them. Most women remain uneasy about "doing it themselves" and pessimistic about women's chances of succeeding in politics. Most women believe that a

*This and the following findings are from Virginia Slims–Harris Setlow Poll, 1972.

woman presidential candidate is not possible for another ten years. Only one out of six women would vote for a woman president (one of three among single and black women). But the die is cast: "There are many signs that women are now playing for keeps in politics more than at any time in the past and that this activism will accelerate. . . . Clearly these results point to a condition of growing confidence, determination, and bitterness that combine to make a potential explosion of woman-power in politics."*

Those who have no power have only one way to get it and that is through those who have it. Unless, of course, violent overthrow is an alternative, and that does not seem either a desirable or a possible alternative in the case of women and men. So women must have the cooperation of men if they are to move into the power-wielding and decision-making bodies of the world. In the long run, it was men who gave women the vote. It was men who passed the Equal Rights Amendment in Congress and who are ratifying it in the states. But it has taken organized political pressure from women to get these things. Even though more and more men are believing in equal rights, and many men are seeing that there are gains for them as well as for women in sharing the responsibility for running the world, as a body men are not likely to move over, or to share the security and power of dominance, without pressure from women.

It is not only in politics that change is both inevitable and necessary. All the institutions of society—education, business, industry, the church—need to make room for women in decision and policy-making capacities.

I can speak most personally about the church. It has been an institution dear to me all my life. Probably if I had been a man thirty years ago I would have chosen it as my profession. Instead I chose to marry a minister! Now I have a hard time going to church. The language, all "he's" and "hims," all the masculine words—"king," "lord," "master,"—the hymns and scriptures that speak only to men: "Rise up, oh men of God." Those are the "little" things. But

*Louis Harris, *Ms.*, July 1972.

they hurt, once your consciousness is raised, and they also reinforce and perpetuate the superiority of males and the inferiority of females. Though the women sit in the pews and do much of the day-to-day work of the church—church schools, office work, fund raising, missions, for example—the power structure is male and the important work in the worship service is done by males. Why aren't more women wanted as ministers? That's a nurturing job! Why shouldn't girls be acolytes? Why shouldn't women be ushers? And if religious education and feeding the hungry are important activities, men should be involved in them too. God is not, after all, a he. God is powerful, judging, just, strong, aggressive—all "masculine" traits—but God is also compassionate, creating, caring, comforting, nurturing, loving—all "feminine" traits. God is neither male nor female; God is both male and female. The valuing of the female in everyone, and in God, would lead to the increased status of women in the church—and, by the same route, to the exaltation of those values that preserve, rather than those that destroy. On this issue as on many others, "The Church is the taillight rather than the headlight," to use Martin Luther King's image.* The small number of men in church pews has long been a concern—the church has not seemed relevant to male concerns of success, achievement, power. Increasingly women too may stay away, not just because the church seems to be irrelevant in social issues, but because it chooses to remain the institution most oppressive to women. When, and if, there are more women in the pulpits, there will be more men in the pews, because it will mean that we are valuing the "feminine" and the "masculine" in both sexes.

The church is the most powerfully repressive institution because it speaks with the voice of God, however perverted that voice may have been by male church dignitaries (I thank thee God, that thou hast not made me a woman). That's why more and more women are feeling that the only way they will ever become part of the institution

*Martin Luther King, Jr., "Letter from a Birmingham Jail," *Christian Century,* 80 (June 12, 1963), 772.

in any significant way is through organized efforts within the church. Recently a woman in a church group to which I had just spoken said, "You know, there's a memorial fund in our church. Most of the money in it was given by women in memory of their husbands. But there are no women on the memorial committee!" Now there's a concrete instance that one woman or a small group of women could rally around to begin to raise consciousness and make changes in a local church. There are hundreds of such instances not only in churches but in all our institutions where women could begin to make significant changes.

Things like that aren't easy for us as women. We are afraid to risk speaking out, afraid of ridicule, afraid of being labeled "aggressive," afraid we'll be called silly. We aren't trained to fight for our rights, except manipulatively. Yet women must learn to think and to act if we are to share the responsibilities and the rewards of equality. It's true that power corrupts, but so does powerlessness. Too many of us as women have been irresponsible and frivolous, and too content with our lot. None of the traditional images of women—passive sweet child, holy mother, seductive temptress, or manipulative witch —demands enough of us as human beings. Most of us want men to move over and give us a chance. Too few of us are willing to take the risks and responsibilities involved in making the chance count.

In this country—or anywhere in the world for that matter—we do not raise either men or women to fulfill their potential, to be able to become the fullest human beings they can. Too many people are not free from hunger and cold and disease. Too many people live under the threat of death from war or pollution or overpopulation. Too many people haven't even the chance to live out the *years* of their lives, much less the human potential. And even those of us who are relatively free from these specters are limited by the narrow definitions of what a woman can be and what a man can be.

It is time that both sexes begin to share more fully both the joys and the burdens that we have traditionally considered the unique role of one or the other. We need to develop a cooperative rather than a ruthlessly competitive society. We must replace the old standards of what is "masculine" and what is "feminine" with a new standard of what is human. Our institutions need to be so structured that everyone can share the service work, the creative work, and the decision-making power so that all people can participate in society at any level they choose and are capable of. We must free men from the rat race of money and success and competition and sexual reputation, and we must free women from the need to be selfless in ways that make them less than persons. We need to affirm and integrate the best of the traditional worlds of both sexes. Both in individuals and in society at large we must affirm an interrelating of the nurturing and the achieving so that all human beings can achieve full humanity.

When we can use every individual thus fully, we will solve the great problems of the world. Of course we cannot wait for that utopia. All the issues must be worked on together. But women and men working together have a better chance of figuring out ways to bring a runaway planet under control for the two reasons that this book is all about—we will increasingly value the nurturing side of both men and women, and we will have the full creativity of half of the human race, which has rarely used its full talents up to now.

I believe that it is not utopian to assume that a meeting in the middle will move us toward the worldwide peace and plenty that humanity has aspired to for hundreds of years. It will also move us toward the racial and ethnic and creedal equality for which we still struggle in vain. The development of a *human identity* will include women and men, black and white, brown and yellow, Jew and Greek, Gentile and Hindu. It is possible that when we are able to develop such a *human identity,* a synthesis of the feminine and the masculine identities, we can turn our inventive and aggressive efforts to the kinds of scientific and technological advances that will re-create the world and our nurturing and compassionate qualities to seeing that everyone everywhere benefits. We will discover that as males and females we are interdependent, that we can become more human together than we can separately. We just don't know what might happen if all men used their hearts as well as their heads and women used their heads as well as their hearts. It's time to find out, and that is the message of this book!

Nine / Living With a "Liberated" Woman:

A Response by Howard J. Clinebell, Jr.

Wherever I go these days, the subject of my changed and changing life as a woman comes up. And nearly always, someone asks, "How does your husband feel about all this?" I decided to ask him to answer that directly this time. Here is his response:

How do I feel about it all? As I reflect on your question I'm aware, and you know, too, that I have a lot of mixed and conflicting feelings about the changes in you and in our marriage. We've had years of meeting on my side of the relationship instead of in the middle. And I'm used to relating to women, especially you, from a one-up position. So this meet in the middle business is rough for me at times. Sometimes I get nostalgic for the "good ol' days"—when I was the sun and you were the willing satellite, doing most of the dirty work and providing all that delicious nurturing when I wanted it.

But then I also get the disquieting awareness that the ol' days weren't as good as I see them through my nostalgic haze. Both of us were paying an exhorbitant price for our one-up, one-down relating. Maybe the best way to get at it is to talk about the gains I now feel as a man married to a more liberated women.

The biggest gain is an increase in positive warmth and closeness based on mutual respect and caring, in contrast to the sticky closeness we used to have. That's where it's at, for me, and it offsets a lot of the pain and sense of loss. I feel more connected since I'm not exploiting you in the many ways I did in the early years and you're not exploiting me in the ways you did.

By exploiting you, I mean taking advantage of your willingness to be taken advantage of by staying in your place as a satellite. Getting rid of the dim awareness that my self-esteem and my doing my thing were made possible by exploiting another human being, you, is a big gain for me. I particularly don't want to be in the position of exploiting someone I care about deeply.

Another gain that's linked to the greater closeness is the increase in honesty and openness that I feel in our marriage. We seem to communicate better about where we really are and there's less of the male-female manipulative gaming that we've always been so good at. That means sex has improved for me, too. I like the fact that you're more openly interested in sex and able to be more active in our mutual pleasuring. Of course, sometimes when my Child side anger gets stirred up by feelings of being deprived of nurturing by you, it gets in the way of good sex. But the upswing in the closeness and caring between us has helped the liveliness of our sex life.

Most of the time I like the fact that we now do our fighting openly and honestly rather than in the manipulative, cold-war ways we were so accomplished at. Living with someone who is using more of herself, as you now are, has many payoffs as well as problems. You're both much more interesting and more difficult to live with than in the early years of our marriage! I feel some regret that you've had a lot of unlived life in you through the years and that you didn't use more of it because of the tight little wife-husband role boxes we put ourselves into. So it's a gain that you're freer.

Another gain for me is feeling much freer of the load of your dependency on me as the primary support for your identity and worth as a person. The fact that you're now sharing the load of feeling some responsibility for earning money also lightens the weight I feel. Of course my reluctance to let go of my male "get ahead" drive raises the point that the burden must have served some function for me. But the main thing is that your new autonomy and self-image have lessened the sticky dependency we both had on each other, and that feels good. It means that we can now *choose* our relationship rather than feel we *have* to have it to survive. That takes the feeling of being trapped away. And although it makes the future less certain and predictable, it makes it also more open and freeing.

The gain that really convinces me that this revolution is mine as well as yours—that it's men's liberation and not just women's—is the unfreezing of some of my feelings. You now have more freedom to *do* things with your intelligence and creativity; but I have a new freedom to *feel* a lot of things my male programming kept me from feeling in the past. I have in mind feelings of tenderness, vulnerability, failure, really needing others, and admitting even to myself how much I hurt at times. The freeing awareness for me is that these aren't "unmasculine" feelings and that rather than being a sign of weakness as a man, being in touch with them enriches my life as a human being and therefore strengthens my inner feelings of real masculinity. Incidentally, hiding my "weak" feelings from you and from myself was a game we both played to keep me looking "strong." Letting go of that saves a lot of energy for more important things. If I can keep moving in that direction it could result in my letting go of some of the heavy demands I put on myself as a male to succeed and achieve. I haven't made much progress on that one yet, but it would be a big load to get rid of.

There's another gain for me that is a mixed one because it didn't happen when our children were younger. Now I know that fathers can and should be as close to children as mothers and that it's great for everybody when it happens. As you know, I feel sad and cheated —as though I've cheated myself—by the way my success-achieve-ment drive (and our shared assumption that mothers were supposed to be the most intimately involved with children) kept me from having as satisfying a relationship with our children during the early years as I could have had. There are some strong regrets around that and a determination to keep working at deepening those relation-ships even though our children are older.

Well, there are also some negative aspects for me of the change in you and in our marriage. As I've said, I do get nostalgic at times; sometimes I think I exaggerate the gains for me in our more liberated marriage and the extent to which I feel liberated inside myself and in our marriage. Even though I know we can't, and *most* of me doesn't want to go back to the old way, I still feel a sense of loss of the safe, familiar ways of relating which we had a lot of practice with in the first two-thirds of our marriage. Part of this is losing the goodies that came from having our marriage revolve around my life and career. I think it's true in most cases, as in ours, that it's the woman who's going to have to take the initiative in changing the balance if she doesn't like the way it is. It's hard to give up all the advantages —or what seem like advantages—of being a male. Sometimes too, when for some reason I feel unsuccessful or insecure in my work, I really miss the automatic self-esteem lift that I used to get from feeling I was on top in our relationship.

The only gain for me that I can see in my sharing the housework is that I understand what a lot you've put up with all these years. Which is a very minor gain! I don't really like making beds and doing dishes, but I do think it's only right for us to share the load. Often I feel resentful and resistant to the whole idea and that's one of the negatives.

There are some other things I don't like about our changes, too. One is that your anger about the put downs and rejections of being a woman seems exaggerated to me sometimes. And I resent the ricocheting anger that often clobbers me. Of course I deserve some of your anger when I revert to my male chauvinist responses, but lots of times I feel I get your anger when I don't deserve it. Of course, it helps to know you're aware of that too. The other side of the anger bit is that whether it's appropriate or not, it's better for our relationship if we let it come out and deal with it honestly rather than letting it log-jam our loving and sexy feelings for each other.

The positive side of this consciousness-raising and awareness of your anger is that I am more aware of the innumerable ways that our society *does* treat you and other women as second-class citizens. It's been amazing to me to discover that we do experience lots of things differently, probably because of the ways we were programmed as a little girl and boy. This discovery is another fringe benefit for me.

Looking back over the last few years or so, I realize that I've alternately resisted, accepted, and encouraged your changes. I guess I've had to adjust to them in little pieces. I've appreciated it when you were aware of how hard it is for me and were tolerant and patient with my need to change gradually. I'm pleased and a little surprised with how far we've come in these years. I'm amazed at how relaxed I feel about things that really threw me a curve when we first encountered them. Like your wanting to use Ms., for example. When you first brought that up I went into orbit, remember? I accused you of not liking our marriage and a lot of other things. I was really threatened. Now I find that I not only see why Ms. is important to you, I actually like using it.

So the negative parts for me of the change in our relationship are acute when I feel you've joined me in the "success" rat race and we don't have enough time together, or we're disconnected or fighting for some reason. I think it would have helped me handle the changes more constructively if I had been in a support group of men whose wives were struggling as you were. You've had a lot of support from other women, but I've felt very much alone in the whole thing. Maybe a couples' group where the wives were changing as you were would have helped. If I had been able to check things out with other husbands, get some perspective on our pain from other couples, it might have eased the transition.

But the strongest single experience for me in all this right now, is that our progress toward a more equal marriage has already produced some very good things. Having had a juicy taste of our new freedom to be ourselves, I want more. That awareness helps to offset the resistances and keeps me working at liberating my side of our relationship. What's always in the background for me is that our relationship is and always has been valuable. That's what I prize and that's what we build on. Oh yes, the difference between our old intimacy based on our Parent-Child needs for each other, and our new intimacy of saying yes to each other—really affirming each other as autonomous, unique persons—that's very different. I'm certain we've a lot of struggles ahead, but the meeting in the middle we've done so far feels good to me. It feels liberating to me as a person, as a man, and as a husband.

Epilogue / What's a Woman to Do?

Time after time a woman says to me, "I'm tired of playing the old games; I'm tired of being second best. I want to do what *I* want to do for a change, but my husband (or boss, or friend, or colleague) won't hear of it. I can't change because he won't." It's a valid statement, but it needs translating. It means, "I'm not ready or willing to risk changing because I might lose the relationship I've got. I might lose my job or my marriage or the security of being liked and accepted by men." There is reality in that. Anyone contemplating change needs to ask herself, "What are the risks and are they worth it?"

But if you are honest in asking the question and in being willing to hear the answers, things often turn out *not* to be as hopeless as you had supposed. Some women discover that the "I can't" means "I'm afraid to and I'm hoping he won't let me because then I won't have to take the risk." It is remarkable how many men *are* willing and even eager (though they still have mixed feelings) to make changes when they discover women are deeply unhappy.

Another question a woman can ask when she becomes aware of dissatisfaction, but feels she can't change, is whether she is dissatisfied with the role she is playing as a woman or with the particular relationship she finds herself in. Of course, those two factors are interrelated, but it helps to sort out which part of it is not liking the person or persons you have to live or work with and which part is not liking the role you have to play. If the relationship is basically good, then it is likely that both people are open to change in order to preserve it. We underestimate most men if we think that they are completely closed to change. Of course they are often threatened and therefore resistant, but then, so are we. A young woman I know felt regularly angry because her boss always took her ideas and presented them as his own. When she got the courage to let him know she felt he was treating her that way because she was a woman (he didn't do that to the men in the organization), he was surprised. It hadn't occurred to him that women like to get credit for their accomplishments too. He valued her work so he was willing to change. Of course, he might have fired her. That's the risk she took.

And that's the back-to-the-wall alternative. Sometimes it *is* true that when a woman decides to change the status quo, the man or men she has to deal with will not tolerate it. Then she simply has to decide whether the relationship is more important than her emancipation or vice versa.

Usually things are not that cut and dried, however, and there are a number of approaches a woman can take if she decides she really does want things to be different. First she needs to become aware of her own motives and her own feelings and to try to discover what she *does* want in the way of change. It helps to talk with other women, friends, or relatives, or to join a consciousness-raising group (or start one—get some of your friends together and start talking about it or write to the national office of NOW* for instructions on how to begin).

Second, it's important to try to be sensitive to what the man or men in her life will feel. If her husband, for example, is resistant, as most men are to some degree, it helps if she can at least try, and let him know she's trying, to understand how painful it is to him. At a gut level, most men feel that women are upsetting the "natural order of things" and that is possibly frightening and certainly uncomfortable. What seems so obvious to a woman who suddenly feels herself *equal* does not seem at all obvious to her husband. Find someplace else to drain off the anger. It only pushes men away. If you've read this book from start to finish, you're aware that I know how difficult that is to do. I'm learning it the hard way.

*National Organization for Women, 1957 East 73rd Street, Chicago, Illinois 60649.

The third step for a woman trying to change things is to do what she has to do in a sensitive way, not an attacking or a rejecting one. If you decide you must have help with the housework or the child care, then present your frustration and anger honestly from your Adult side, rather than attacking with your Parent side (Why can't you carry more of the load around here?) or whiningly from your Child side (You just don't care whether I'm happy or not). Those are attacking remarks that put men on the defensive. An Adult approach might be, "Look, I know it's hard for you, too, but I'm feeling really frustrated these days because there's so much I want to do besides housework and raising children. Can you help out or do you think we should hire some help?" Or whatever other alternatives might present themselves.

All of which sounds just lovely, but of course it doesn't always work. Try it first and see whether your husband or boss or colleague will respond. If he doesn't respond after your fair and reasonable approach, then maybe you just have to get angry. "Can't you hear me? I'm angry and unhappy and I'm just not willing to put up with things the way they are any more!" That's an Adult approach if it's nonmanipulative and honest. The important thing here is to use your strength in a straightforward way. The old ways of stealthy manipulation or domineering control don't get us where we want to go. The power we have is in the need of both women and men for each other. Neither sex need be the helpless victim of the other. "Saying it straight" is usually far more effective in gaining cooperation from another person. At that point some men take notice. "Gee, I didn't know you felt so strongly!" Others attack. "So get lost. I'm the boss around here!"

So what's a woman to do? It's certainly a risk. A woman then has to decide either that the relationship isn't worth it and she'll make it on her own, or that she'll retreat for awhile, or take another tack. It is often true that in such a marriage, for example, when the husband is not willing to consider change, a woman can make many changes on her own. She can simply begin doing things differently. She can make gradual changes hoping that her husband will come to the place where he can accept more significant change. Many men do. If there are small children and little money, then a woman may be effectively trapped. Maybe she has to bide her time, or get some counseling, or try a different approach. Certainly she can find herself a group of women who are interested in the same issues. Sooner or later she will have to decide whether the relationship is worth what it demands of her. There is simply no one solution for all women. Each of us has to find what's right for us. And it isn't easy in any circumstance.

If women who are contemplating a marriage or job or other relationship with a man want a relationship of equality, they would do well to thrash out these matters ahead of time. An awful lot of pain can be avoided if both partners know what they're getting into and decide it's worth it. Knowing the other person's expectations ahead of time can save a lot of grief.

As women and men we demand a lot from each other these days. We demand a lot from marriage. Women are now expecting men to be not only good providers but good family men too. It behooves us as women to demand as much from ourselves. Are we reciprocating in our own development? Are we willing to give up helplessness and dependence or manipulative power in order to meet men as equals? We can't wait for other women to take up the cause for us. We can't wait for men to say, "Hey I'm ready to move over and make room for you on an equal basis." It won't happen, either in our individual lives or collectively. What we have got to say now as women is, "Okay, I'll do it myself!" We cannot be loathe to take responsibility or to commit ourselves. We must be willing to see ourselves as responsible for the world outside the home if we want men to see us that way. Unfortunately, it is still true that only a small minority of women are the ones who participate in community concerns either on a volunteer basis or otherwise. Too many of us still spend too much of our time playing bridge or coffee-klatching.

The traditional image of women does not demand enough of us as human beings or as women. I repeat my conviction that that doesn't mean all women should go to work outside the home. All of us, women and men, need to discover who we are as human beings, apart from whatever it is we *do.* What it does mean is that women must *feel* and *take* equal responsibility for the way the world runs, however they decide to do it. The anger in Women's Liberation is a demand for a *better* relationship, not for *no* relationship with men.

Now that I am coming to the end of these pages, the question with which I began so many months ago returns to me. "What will I be when I grow up?" What of my journey through life? What of my feelings now about myself and my sense of worth? Are the issues any clearer, the questions any more pertinent, the answers any more satisfying? I have found out several things. I've discovered a lot more accumulated anger than I knew was there. It has helped to spew some of it out on paper, to refine it, to try it by fire, to understand it, to be rid of it. And I am rid of much of it, though much remains, and will, as long as women are second-clsss citizens. But it is tempered now, and as often as not directed at myself for not using the power I have, for wasting valuable time in frustration and laziness, in blaming others for my failures and inadequacies, for insisting on seeing myself as helpless, inadequate, and worthless. Sometimes, still, it's difficult for me to let go of the old "I can't" feelings.

But I've found some answers too. One is that I've misinterpreted my discontent, restlessness, doubt, despair, and longing as things to limit me rather than as signs that it was time to grow and change. I've discovered how many things I want to do, how many things I can do, and that I have the power to do some of them instead of spending time and energy stewing because I never did them before.

"Time as measured is the enemy of time as lived."* A friend of mine recently died of cancer. She was about my age—a busy, alive person with many plans for her own growth and fulfillment in middle age—when she realized that she had not long to live. She experienced deep despair and anger that she could not live out her life. But she never let the despair and anger get in the way of living fully as long as she lived and of doing what she wanted and was able to do as long as she could. When she wanted to do something, she did

*Robert MacIver, *The Challenge of the Passing Years* (New York: Simon & Schuster, 1962), p. xxiv.

it now, rather than moaning that she couldn't, or that something prevented her, or that there were so many things she wanted to do she couldn't do all of them. She said, "The important thing is to live the time you have."

I am grateful to Lois for herself and for those words. They inspire me to do and be what I can in the time that I have, to enjoy the now rather than wasting energy on regrets for the past, to make the future count however long or short it may be for me.

Wherever a woman is in her "passage through time," if she is twenty or forty or sixty or eighty, such an attitude can be helpful. It is true that we are limited in many ways as human beings, perhaps particularly as women, by circumstances of all kinds—physical, emotional, spiritual. But we are not as dependent on those circumstances as we like to believe we are. We can live fully if we choose to, though it takes courage and strength. Living fully doesn't mean we can have everything we want. We can't stop time, nor change all the injustices that limit us within our lifetimes.

But we can give up banging our heads against the stone wall of reality. I have not got another lifetime to live and I can't relive the one I've had. Equality between the sexes may not arrive while I live and I can't convince everyone that it should. But I can break out of my own box; I can help to change *some* things for myself and for others. And it isn't that hard to know the difference between what I can change and what I can't.

What will I be when I grow up? I don't even need the question any more. For being grown up is not having arrived at a particular place emotionally or spiritually or chronologically. It is living as fully as possible in the time that I have. It means making new choices constantly, making mistakes, trying again, discovering new directions, finding new areas of life as yet unexplored. It means sorting out which are the "demons" within and without which I must fight with all my might, and which are the red herrings that are irrelevant to the struggle. What shall I be now that I'm grown up? Me, that's what. And that's good—and makes meeting in the middle good.

73 74 75 76 77 10 9 8 7 6 5 4 3 2 1